BOB DYLAN THE LYRICS 196

FOREVER Y
永远年轻

鲍勃·迪伦诗歌集 1961—2020
VOL.06

[美] 鲍勃·迪伦 著　李皖 译

中信出版集团 | 北京

行星波
PLANET WAVES

在这样一个夜里	7
走,走,走了	11
苦难的妈妈	15
黑榛	19
你身上有种东西	21
永远年轻	25
挽歌	29
你,天使你	33
永不说再见	37
婚礼之歌	41

——— 附加歌词 ———

除了你	45

轨道上的血
BLOOD ON THE TRACKS

忧郁中纠结万端	55
命运的简单戏法	65
你现在是个大女孩了	69
愚蠢的风	73
你走了会让我寂寞	81
早上来见我	87

目录

莉莉、罗斯玛丽和红心杰克	91
如果你见到她,问声好	101
暴风雨中的避难所	105
倾盆的雨	111

―――― 附加歌词 ――――

得我来	115
呼号蓝调	123

渴望
DESIRE

飓风	133
伊西丝	143
莫桑比克	149
再喝一杯咖啡(下面的溪谷)	151
哦,姐姐	155
乔伊	157
杜兰戈罗曼史	167
黑钻石湾	175
萨拉	183

―――― 附加歌词 ――――

被遗弃的爱	189
鲇鱼	193
金纺车	199

丽塔·梅	203
七天	207
手语	211
金钱蓝调	215

PLANET WA[V]

PLANET WAVES
行星波

在这样一个夜里

走，走，走了

苦难的妈妈

黑桩

你身上有种东西

永远年轻

挽歌

你，天使你

永不说再见

婚礼之歌

附加歌词

除了你

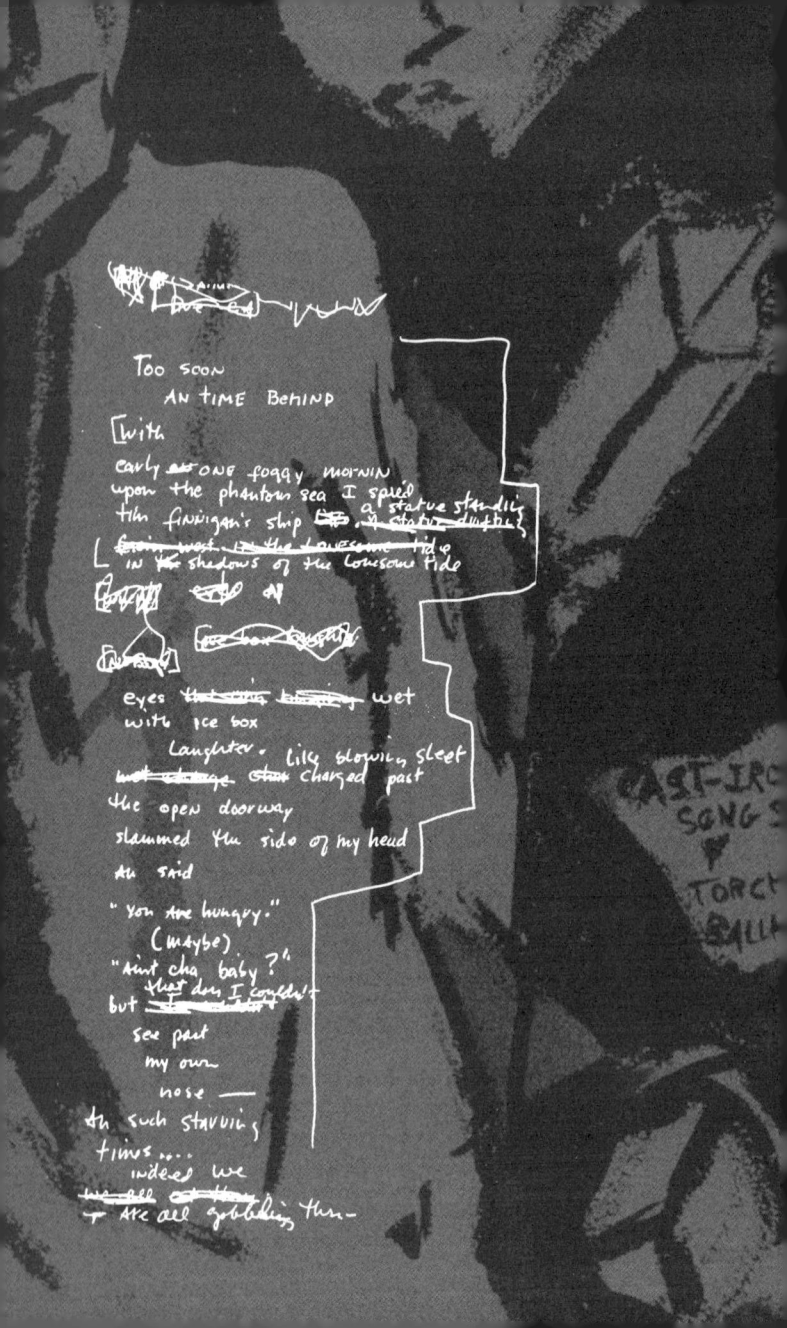

TOO SOON
   AN TIME BEHIND
[with
early one foggy mornin
upon the phantom sea I spied
tim finnigan's ship a statue standing
in the shadows of the lonesome tide

eyes wet
with ice box
     Laughter. lily blowin sleet
charged past
the open doorway
slammed the side of my head
an said
"you are hungry."
   (maybe)
"Aint cha baby?"
but I couldn't
see past
my own
   nose —
in such starving
times.... indeed we
+ are all gobbling thru—

《行星波》是迪伦第 14 张录音室专辑,于 1974 年 1 月 17 日由庇护所唱片公司(Asylum Records)发行,与上一张原创专辑相隔 3 年半。"行星波"是个地球物理学名词,指由于地转参数随着纬度的变化而产生的大尺度大气波动。

这张专辑录制于 1973 年 11 月 2、5、6、8、9 和 14 日,共录了 6 场。有一点很奇特——这是一张没有制作人的专辑。所有歌曲都是现场即兴表演录制而成,迪伦和"乐队"诸友给予了彼此完全的信任。专辑中的歌曲是精确合奏的奇迹,"好像这些家伙可以在睡梦中尾随迪伦"。

此时迪伦举家搬迁,从美国东部的纽约搬到了西部加州的马里布。他换了唱片公司,因不满合约条款,与合作 12 年的哥伦比亚唱片公司了断,转投到了庇护所唱片公司旗下。

专辑制作的同时,迪伦与"乐队"启动了自 1966 年以来已停滞 8 年的巡演。

这张专辑大体上由两类内容构成:少部分是迪伦对家乡以及少年时代的回忆(《你身上有种东西》,附加歌词《除了你》);大部分是"火炬歌谣"——这是爵士乐中的概念,指经历了巨大煎熬,像火炬般猛烈燃烧的情歌。

多数情歌都写给萨拉,有一首写给迪伦少年时代的情人。表面看,它们与前面专辑——《纳什维尔天际线》和《新晨》类似。但听众们很快就发现,这些情歌是温柔与哀泣之作,与之前那种安稳很不一样。

《黑榛》表现了青涩的爱,是迪伦写给在希宾小城时女友的歌。它的美来自过去,或者说,来自挥之不去、余音绕梁的一切。正因为它已逝去,那里有一个少年不可挽回的柔软内心。与之同理,《你身上有种东西》有更为深厚的这类情绪。迪伦有一种手法是"不写",白描之外,经常有潜台词。

《永不说再见》有令人印象深刻的冷寂和空旷,虽然也并没有几笔真正写到这些。它并非简单的情诗,里面隐伏着变故和变化,好像是正向的,但终究并不清楚是好变化还是坏变化。

《苦难的妈妈》写性爱。在专辑中表现如此猛烈的性爱是第二次,上一次还是十年前,在《西班牙哈莱姆事件》中。它一开始用黑人布鲁斯的行话入题,很快变成兰波和超现实主义影响下的混合体。这首歌绚丽又刺目,克林顿·海林指出,迪伦在演唱时,用了"他最粗俗(raunchiest)的一种声音"。

《婚礼之歌》明明白白是写给萨拉的。古今中外都难以找到类似的一首诗,将对妻子的爱写得这般疯狂和绝对。这本身蕴藏了不安,像是欠了她巨大的情债。第6节宣布"再造整个世界从不是我的事/宣布冲锋也不是我的本意",迪伦终于切入他直面的困境:相较于社会期待他"做改变世界的人"，他更看重做好丈夫和好父亲。

《挽歌》是写给萨拉吗？应该不是。但它也有爱到极处的心理："我恨我自己爱你和由此暴露的弱点。"罕有评论家分析这首似乎如此具体、真实的作品究竟是在写什么。它是杰作，直到写出、录制出的那一刻，歌手仍深度迷陷在那个梦魇般的事件中。确实，它很像是在表达艺术家对他的缪斯和听众的爱恨交缠之意。迪伦的钢琴弹奏与歌曲十分相配，令评论家们赞叹。海林认为，《挽歌》是自摩托事故以来迪伦最扭曲的歌，代表了他相当惊人的宣泄。

在不祥信息的指引下，一些评论还发现，《走，走，走了》隐含着自杀意图。为了避免听众这样解读，迪伦后来改了词。

然而，以上所有这些，与《永远年轻》比起来，都可以忽略不计。这首在迪伦脑海中萦绕了5年的歌，甫一诞生即光芒四射，随着1974年的巡演迅速成了名曲。这是内心里的父亲写给孩子的寄语，充满了最深切的殷殷祝福。诗人金斯堡认为"这首歌充满了希望，毫不玄奥，显然鼓励着人们去找寻属于自己的真理"，"应给每个国家每所学校的每个孩子在每天早晨歌唱"。

《永远年轻》的力量，在我看来也来自幻灭。光明巨大，乃是因为其背后有巨大的黑暗。所有迪伦寄予希望的，都是现实未成的，那是人类最简单、最直白却又是最难实现的正义。

此前的第13张录音室专辑《迪伦》是一张非原创作品专辑，由哥伦比亚唱片公司于1973年11月16日发行。

ON A NIGHT LIKE THIS

On a night like this
So glad you came around
Hold on to me so tight
And heat up some coffee grounds
We got much to talk about
And much to reminisce
It sure is right
On a night like this

On a night like this
So glad you've come to stay
Hold on to me, pretty miss
Say you'll never go away to stray
Run your fingers down my spine
Bring me a touch of bliss
It sure feels right
On a night like this

On a night like this
I can't get any sleep
The air is so cold outside
And the snow's so deep

在这样一个夜里

在这样一个夜里
很高兴你来
将我抱这么紧
我们把咖啡末加热
有好多话要说
有好多事回忆
这真好
在这样一个夜里

在这样一个夜里
很高兴你留下来
抱着我,美人儿
告诉我你永远不会离开
你的手指滑下我的脊骨
带给我丝丝狂喜
这感觉真好
在这样一个夜里

在这样一个夜里
我没有了睡意
外面天这么冷
积雪这样深

Build a fire, throw on logs
And listen to it hiss
And let it burn, burn, burn, burn
On a night like this

Put your body next to mine
And keep me company
There is plenty a-room for all
So please don't elbow me

Let the four winds blow
Around this old cabin door
If I'm not too far off
I think we did this once before
There's more frost on the window glass
With each new tender kiss
But it sure feels right
On a night like this

生起火来吧,扔进木柴
听那嘶嘶声响起
让它燃烧、燃烧、燃烧、燃烧
在这样一个夜里

将身体挨着我吧
且陪在我身旁
这里地方够大
请不要用胳膊推搡

就让四方的风
吹打这老木屋的门
如果我不是太健忘
我想我们有过这么一次
随着一个个温柔新吻
霜花在窗玻璃一朵朵开放
这感觉真好啊
在这样一个夜里

GOING, GOING, GONE

I've just reached a place
Where the willow don't bend
There's not much more to be said
It's the top of the end
I'm going
I'm going
I'm gone

I'm closin' the book
On the pages and the text
And I don't really care
What happens next
I'm just going
I'm going
I'm gone

I been hangin' on threads
I been playin' it straight
Now, I've just got to cut loose

走，走，走了[1]

我刚来到一个地方
这儿的柳树不会弯
没什么好说的
这就是结束的顶点
我继续走
我继续走
我走了

我合上这部书
合上了书页和文字
我真的并不在意
那后续如何
我只是继续走
我继续走
我走了

我一直悬在索上
我一直绷得笔直
现在，我必须斩断它了

---

[1] 标题"Going, Going, Gone"，既是拍卖落槌时确认成交的提示语，亦是对棒球被击飞将要全垒打时的形容。

Before it gets late
So I'm going
I'm going
I'm gone

Grandma said, "Boy, go and follow your heart
And you'll be fine at the end of the line
All that's gold isn't meant to shine
Don't you and your one true love ever part"

I been walkin' the road
I been livin' on the edge
Now, I've just got to go
Before I get to the ledge
So I'm going
I'm just going
I'm gone

趁着不是太迟
所以我继续走
我继续走
我走了

奶奶说:"孩子,去吧,追随你的心
到那条路最后,你会没事
不是所有金子都注定发光
不要与你唯一的真爱分离"

我一直走在这路上
我一直活在这边缘
现在,我得走了
趁着还没到悬崖边
所以我继续走
我只是继续走
我走了

TOUGH MAMA

Tough Mama, meat shakin' on your bones
I'm gonna go down to the river and get some stones
Sister's on the highway with that steel-drivin' crew
Papa's in the big house, his workin' days are through
Tough Mama, can I blow a little smoke on you?

Dark Lady, won't you move it on over and make some room?
Rollin' steady, sweepin' through the country like a broom
Put your arms around me, like a circle 'round the sun
You got a pocket full of money but you can't help me none
Shady Lady, the dress that you are wearin' weighs a ton

Angel Baby, born of a blinding light and a changing wind
Drive me crazy, you know who you are and where you've been
Starin' at the ceiling, standin' on the chair
Big fires blazing, ashes in the air
Angel Baby, I wonder what you done back there

I'm crestfallen—the world of illusion is at my door
I hear you callin', same old thing like it was before

苦难的妈妈

苦难的妈妈,肉在你骨头上抖
我要去河边弄些石头
姐姐在公路和那个钢铁司机一起
爸爸在大房子[1],结束了劳作的日子
苦难的妈妈,我可否将一缕轻烟吹向你?

黑暗女士,你就不会移走它,腾出点地方吗?
稳稳地卷过去,就像扫帚横扫田野
用双臂抱着我吧,有如轨道环绕巨日
腰缠万贯,于我却毫无助益
影夫人,你身上的裙子足足有一吨

天使贝贝,生于炫目的光和变幻的风
使我疯狂,你知道自己是谁,所经何处
瞪着天花板,站在椅子上
大火熊熊,灰烬飞舞空中
天使贝贝,我很想知道你都做了什么

我灰心又丧气——幻想世界就在门口
我听见了你在呼唤,情形一如往昔

---

[1] 大房子,俚语中指监狱。

Crawlin' through the meadow like a lion in the den
Headin' for the round-up at the rainbow's end
Tough Mama, let's get on the road again

像狮穴中的狮子,缓缓走过草地
前往彩虹的尽头聚集
苦难的妈妈,且让我们再次上路

HAZEL

Hazel, dirty-blonde hair
I wouldn't be ashamed to be seen with you anywhere
You got something I want plenty of
Ooh, a little touch of your love

Hazel, stardust in your eye
You're goin' somewhere and so am I
I'd give you the sky high above
Ooh, for a little touch of your love

Oh no, I don't need any reminder
To know how much I really care
But it's just making me blinder and blinder
Because I'm up on a hill and still you're not there

Hazel, you called and I came
Now don't make me play this waiting game
You've got something I want plenty of
Ooh, a little touch of your love

黑榛 [1]

黑榛,金棕色的发
被人看见与你形影不离并不可耻
你有我渴求之物
啊,一点点你的爱意

黑榛,星尘在你眼中
你想去一个地方,我也一样
我愿将高高在上的天穹给你
啊,为一点点你的爱意

啊不,我不需要什么提示
提醒我究竟多在乎
这只会让我的盲目更盲目
因为我已登上山顶而你未至

黑榛,你电话一招我就到
别再与我玩等待的游戏
你拥有我渴求之物
啊,一点点你的爱意

---

[1] Hazel,女名黑兹尔,它的词义是榛树。黑榛与黑兹尔发音相近,用于诗中韵律更合。

SOMETHING THERE IS ABOUT YOU

Something there is about you that strikes a match in me
Is it the way your body moves or is it the way your hair blows free?
Or is it because you remind me of something that used to be
Somethin' that crossed over from another century?

Thought I'd shaken the wonder and the phantoms of my youth
Rainy days on the Great Lakes, walkin' the hills of old Duluth
There was me and Danny Lopez, cold eyes, black night and then there was Ruth
Something there is about you that brings back a long-forgotten truth

Suddenly I found you and the spirit in me sings
Don't have to look no further, you're the soul of many things
I could say that I'd be faithful, I could say it in one sweet, easy breath
But to you that would be cruelty and to me it surely would be death

你身上有种东西

你身上有种东西,擦亮了我心中的火柴
是你头发飘动的样子,还是你身体的
　姿态?
还是你让我想起了曾经的事
那些事从另一个世纪穿越而来?

想来我已怀疑我青春的奇迹和幻影
雨天在五大湖,行走在老德卢斯[1]的山中
有我和丹妮·洛佩兹,冷的眼,黑的夜,然后是
　露丝
你身上有种东西,唤回了遗忘已久
　的事

忽然间我发现了你,我的心灵唱起了歌
无须再多看,你是众多事物的魂魄
我可以说我是忠实的,可以甜蜜、轻松地一口气
　说出
但于你那会是残忍,于我则是
　必死无疑

---

[1] 德卢斯,迪伦的家乡,明尼苏达州城市。

Something there is about you that moves with style and grace
I was in a whirlwind, now I'm in some better place
My hand's on the sabre and you've picked up the baton
Somethin' there is about you that I can't quite put my finger on

你身上有种东西，入时而雅致
昔日我卷入旋风，而今我进入佳境
我手按着弯刀，你拿起了指挥棒
你身上有种东西，我不是太能指明

FOREVER YOUNG

May God bless and keep you always
May your wishes all come true
May you always do for others
And let others do for you
May you build a ladder to the stars
And climb on every rung
May you stay forever young
Forever young, forever young
May you stay forever young

May you grow up to be righteous
May you grow up to be true
May you always know the truth
And see the lights surrounding you
May you always be courageous
Stand upright and be strong
May you stay forever young
Forever young, forever young
May you stay forever young

May your hands always be busy
May your feet always be swift

永远年轻

但愿上帝始终护佑你
但愿你的梦想都能成真
但愿你始终助人
而人人助你
但愿你能造架星辰之梯
并登上它的每一级
但愿你能永远年轻
永远年轻,永远年轻
但愿你能永远年轻

但愿你长成正直的人
但愿你长成真诚的人
但愿你总能知晓真相
看见环绕你的光芒
但愿你总能充满勇气
昂首挺立,无比坚强
但愿你能永远年轻
永远年轻,永远年轻
但愿你能永远年轻

但愿你始终双手不停
但愿你始终脚步轻盈

May you have a strong foundation
When the winds of changes shift
May your heart always be joyful
May your song always be sung
May you stay forever young
Forever young, forever young
May you stay forever young

但愿你的根基稳固
当面对世间那变幻的风
但愿你内心始终欢乐
而你的歌一直被人传颂
但愿你能永远年轻
永远年轻，永远年轻
但愿你能永远年轻

DIRGE

I hate myself for lovin' you and the weakness that it showed
You were just a painted face on a trip down Suicide Road
The stage was set, the lights went out all around the old hotel
I hate myself for lovin' you and I'm glad the curtain fell

I hate that foolish game we played and the need that was expressed
And the mercy that you showed to me, who ever would have guessed?
I went out on Lower Broadway and I felt that place within
That hollow place where martyrs weep and angels play with sin

Heard your songs of freedom and man forever stripped
Acting out his folly while his back is being whipped
Like a slave in orbit, he's beaten 'til he's tame
All for a moment's glory and it's a dirty, rotten shame

There are those who worship loneliness, I'm not one of them

挽歌

我恨我自己爱你和由此暴露的弱点
你不过是《自杀之路》[1]中一张化妆的脸
结局已定,老旅馆四周灯火已熄
我恨我自己爱你,幸好大幕关闭

我恨这愚蠢的游戏,恨这表达的
　需要
还有你对我的怜悯,谁能
　猜到?
我离开下百老汇[2],却感觉人还在那里
那个空无之地,殉道者垂泪,天使与罪恶嬉戏

听到你的歌,关于自由和被剥光的人
每当他后背被鞭打,他便表现他的愚蠢
就像上了道的奴隶,他被殴打到驯服
一切皆为一时之荣耀,这是何其肮脏、恶臭的屈辱

有的人崇拜孤独,我不是这种人

---

[1] 《自杀之路》是迪伦观看的某部剧,通篇可能阐述了迪伦观看这部剧的感受。
[2] 下百老汇,美国纳什维尔的著名表演街区。

In this age of fiberglass I'm searching for a gem
The crystal ball up on the wall hasn't shown me nothing yet
I've paid the price of solitude, but at last I'm out of debt

Can't recall a useful thing you ever did for me
'Cept pat me on the back one time when I was on my knees
We stared into each other's eyes 'til one of us would break
No use to apologize, what diff'rence would it make?

So sing your praise of progress and of the Doom Machine
The naked truth is still taboo whenever it can be seen
Lady Luck, who shines on me, will tell you where I'm at
I hate myself for lovin' you, but I should get over that

在这个玻璃钢的年代,我还在寻找宝石
墙上的水晶球尚未给我显示
我为孤独付出了代价,但最终我已还清债务

想不起你为我做过有用的事
除了有次我跪下时,你拍了拍我的背
我们凝视着彼此的眼,直到有一方崩溃
道歉没有用,那有什么不同?

所以歌颂进步和"末日机器"吧
赤裸裸的真相只要能被看到,依然是禁忌
照耀着我的幸运女神,会告诉你我在哪里
我恨我自己爱你,但我会克服这一点

YOU ANGEL YOU

You angel you
You got me under your wing
The way you walk and the way you talk
I feel I could almost sing

You angel you
You're as fine as anything's fine
The way you walk and the way you talk
It sure plays on my mind

You know I can't sleep at night for trying
Never did feel this way before
I get up at night and walk the floor
If this is love then gimme more
And more and more and more and more

You angel you
You're as fine as can be
The way you smile like a sweet baby child
It just falls all over me

You know I can't sleep at night for trying

你,天使你

你,天使你
你张开羽翼遮护我
你走路和说话的样子
我觉得我简直能唱成歌

你,天使你
你如此美好,如同万物
你走路和说话的样子
确实在我脑海中播出

你知道我晚上睡不着
这种感觉未曾有过
我深夜醒来,在屋中徘徊
假如这就是爱,那么给我更多
更多更多更多更多

你,天使你
你如此美好,不可能更好
你的笑像甜甜的婴孩
只落在我身上

你知道我晚上睡不着

Never did feel this way before
Never did get up and walk the floor
If this is love then gimme more
And more and more and more

You angel you
You got me under your wing
The way you walk and the way you talk
It says everything

这种感觉未曾有过
从未这样醒来,在屋中徘徊
假如这就是爱,那么给我更多
更多更多更多更多

你,天使你
你张开羽翼遮护我
你走路和说话的样子
道出了世间万物

NEVER SAY GOODBYE

Twilight on the frozen lake
North wind about to break
On footprints in the snow
Silence down below

You're beautiful beyond words
You're beautiful to me
You can make me cry
Never say goodbye

Time is all I have to give
You can have it if you choose
With me you can live
Never say goodbye

My dreams are made of iron and steel
With a big bouquet
Of roses hanging down
From the heavens to the ground

The crashing waves roll over me
As I stand upon the sand

永不说再见

暮光映在冰封湖面
北风即将吹散
雪地上的足印
下面一片寂静

你的美超出语言
你的美对我而言
你能让我哭
永不说再见

时光是我能给予的一切
你可以拥有它,只要你选择
你可以跟我一起生活
永不说再见

我的梦是钢铁铸就
带着一大束玫瑰
从青天
垂向地面

汹涌的海浪翻卷
我站在沙滩上

Wait for you to come
And grab hold of my hand

Oh, baby, baby, baby blue
You'll change your last name, too
You've turned your hair to brown
Love to see it hangin' down

等着你来
抓住我的手

啊,宝宝,宝宝,蓝宝宝
你也会将姓氏改换
你已经换成了棕色头发
喜欢看它披垂而下

WEDDING SONG

I love you more than ever, more than time and more than love
I love you more than money and more than the stars above
Love you more than madness, more than waves upon the sea
Love you more than life itself, you mean that much to me

Ever since you walked right in, the circle's been complete
I've said goodbye to haunted rooms and faces in the street
To the courtyard of the jester which is hidden from the sun
I love you more than ever and I haven't yet begun

You breathed on me and made my life a richer one to live
When I was deep in poverty you taught me how to give
Dried the tears up from my dreams and pulled me from the hole
Quenched my thirst and satisfied the burning in my soul

You gave me babies one, two, three, what is more, you saved my life
Eye for eye and tooth for tooth, your love cuts like a knife
My thoughts of you don't ever rest, they'd kill me if I lie

婚礼之歌 [1]

我爱你超乎以往,超乎时光超乎爱情
我爱你超乎金钱,也超乎头顶的星空
爱你超乎疯狂,超乎海上的浪
爱你超乎生命本身,你对我的意义就是这样

自你径直走进来,生命的圆得以圆满
作别了闹鬼房间和街上的脸
还有弄臣躲避太阳的院子
爱你超乎以往,而我还没有开始

你的呼吸吹着我,使这生命更为丰盈
你教我如何给予,当我深陷于贫穷
擦去梦中泪水,拉我走出
 泥潭
解去那焦渴,满足我灵魂中的熊熊烈焰

你赐给我孩子,一个、两个、三个,更好的是,
 你拯救了我的生活
以眼还眼,以牙还牙,你的爱宛如刀割
我对你的思念从不休止,若我说谎,它们会宰了我

---

[1] 本篇由杨盈盈校译。

I'd sacrifice the world for you and watch my senses die

The tune that is yours and mine to play upon this earth
We'll play it out the best we know, whatever it is worth
What's lost is lost, we can't regain what went down in the flood
But happiness to me is you and I love you more than blood

It's never been my duty to remake the world at large
Nor is it my intention to sound a battle charge
'Cause I love you more than all of that with a love that doesn't bend
And if there is eternity I'd love you there again

Oh, can't you see that you were born to stand by my side
And I was born to be with you, you were born to be my bride
You're the other half of what I am, you're the missing piece
And I love you more than ever with that love that doesn't cease

You turn the tide on me each day and teach my eyes to see
Just bein' next to you is a natural thing for me
And I could never let you go, no matter what goes on
'Cause I love you more than ever now that the past is gone

我愿将世界献祭给你,而眼见着我的感觉消失

那曲调属于你也属于我,它在这星球奏响
我们尽己所知弹奏着,无论其价值几何
失去的业已失去,洪水冲走的无从挽回
但我的幸福就是你,我对你的爱浓于血水

再造整个世界从不是我的事
宣布冲锋也不是我的本意
因我爱你超过这一切,这一份爱
　绝不妥协
如果真有来世,我会爱你,再一次

啊,难道你看不出来,你生来就要站我这边
我生来就要与你为伴,你生来就是我的新娘子
你是我的另一半,你是我缺失的部分
而我爱你超乎以往,这份爱永不止息

你每天为我扭转潮头,教我双眼看见
只要在你身边就是自然而然
而我无法让你离开,无论发生什么
因我爱你超乎以往,既然过去已成过去

NOBODY 'CEPT YOU

There's nothing 'round here I believe in
'Cept you, yeah you
And there's nothing to me that's sacred
'Cept you, yeah you

You're the one that reaches me
You're the one that I admire
Every time we meet together
My soul feels like it's on fire
Nothing matters to me
And there's nothing I desire
'Cept you, yeah you

Nothing 'round here I care to try for
'Cept you, yeah you
Got nothing left to live or die for
'Cept you, yeah you

There's a hymn I used to hear
In the churches all the time
Make me feel so good inside
So peaceful, so sublime

除了你

这儿的一切我都不信
除了你,对除了你
也没什么于我是神圣的
除了你,对除了你

你是抵达我的那个
你是我钦敬的那个
每次我们相见
我的灵魂都像腾起大火
什么我都不在乎
什么我都不渴慕
除了你,对除了你

这儿的一切我都不谋求
除了你,对除了你
再没什么堪为之生死
除了你,对除了你

过去我常听到首赞美诗
在教堂里的每时每分
让我内心如此美好
如此庄严,如此宁静

And there's nothing to remind me of that
Old familiar chime
'Cept you, uh huh you

Used to play in the cemetery
Dance and sing and run when I was a child
Never seemed strange
But now I just pass mournfully by
That place where the bones of life are piled
I know somethin' has changed
I'm a stranger here and no one sees me
'Cept you, yeah you

Nothing much matters or seems to please me
'Cept you, yeah you
Nothing hypnotizes me
Or holds me in a spell
Everything runs by me
Just like water from a well
Everybody wants my attention
Everybody's got something to sell
'Cept you, yeah you

再没什么能让我想起
那古老而熟悉的钟声
除了你,嗯除了你

以前我常在墓地玩儿
跳舞、唱歌、奔跑,我是个小孩子
从不觉得奇怪
而现在,我只会悲哀地经过
那人间堆积白骨之所
我知道有些东西变了
我在此地是异乡人,人人视而不见
除了你,对除了你

再没什么紧要事,会使我愉悦
除了你,对除了你
没有什么能催眠我
或者让我着魔
万事皆由我掌控
就像水出自水井
人人都想引起我注意
人人都有东西要兜售
除了你,对除了你

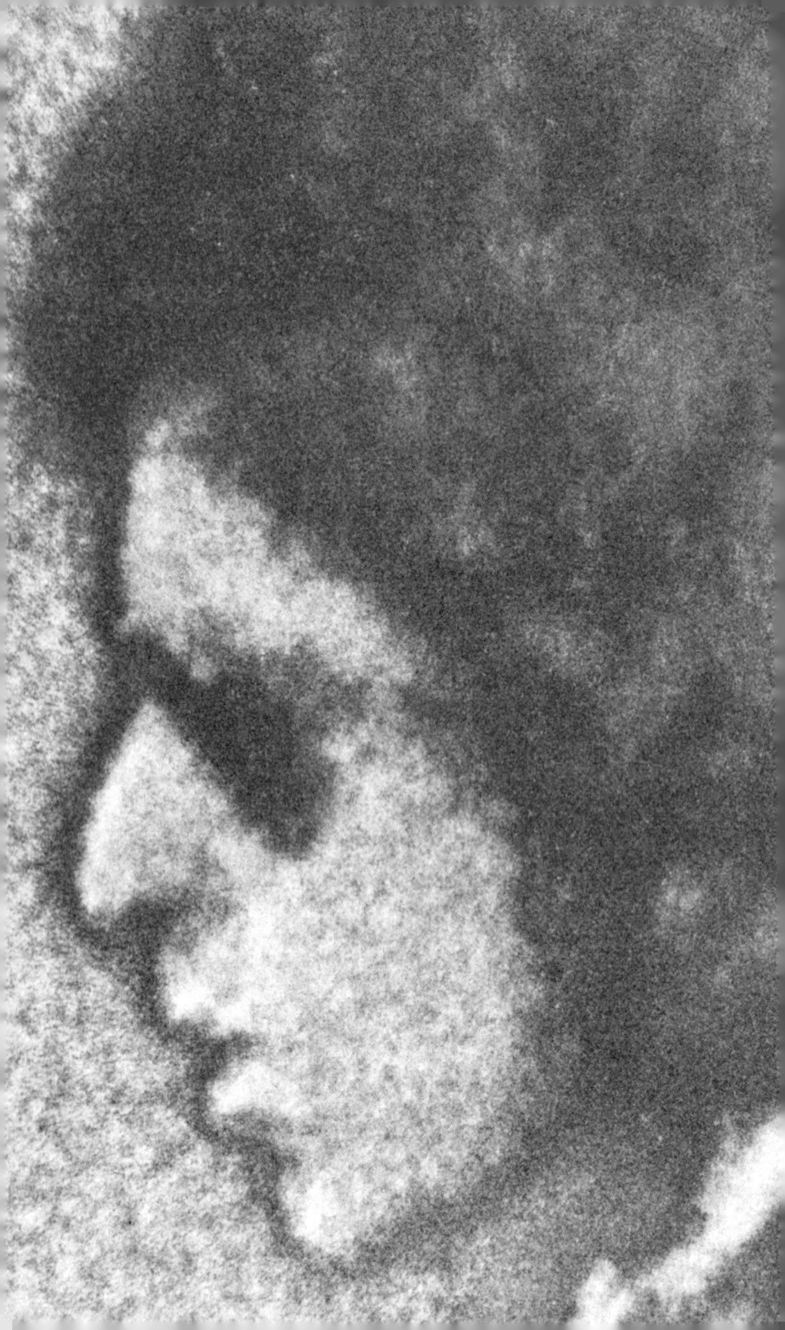

BLOOD ON THE TRACKS
轨道上的血

忧郁中纠结万端

命运的简单戏法

你现在是个大女孩了

愚蠢的风

你走了会让我寂寞

早上来见我

莉莉、罗斯玛丽和红心杰克

如果你见到她,问声好

暴风雨中的避难所

倾盆的雨

附加歌词

得我来 呼号蓝调

(1) Early one mornin', the sun was shining, he was lyin in bed
   [5 in the]
Wonderin' if she'd changed at all, wondering if her hair was still red
Her folks they said their lives together sure was gonna be rough
Never did like Mama's home-made dress, Papa's bankbook wasn't big enough
And he was walking by the side of the road
Rain falling on his shoes
Heading out for the ol' East Coast
Lord knows he paid some dues
Tryin' to get thr — Tangled up in BLUE

1974年,迪伦结束了与庇护所唱片公司的合约,回到哥伦比亚唱片公司。《轨道上的血》是他的第15张录音室专辑,发行于1975年1月20日。

此时迪伦与萨拉的婚姻触礁,《轨道上的血》表现了爱情失败的巨大痛苦。评论界纠结于这张专辑是不是自传,但迪伦否认了其自传性。

1973年,迪伦一家搬到西部马里布后,他和萨拉的关系开始恶化。次年1月,迪伦重启巡演,再次上路让他的老毛病都回来了——女人、酒、大麻、动不动发脾气。萨拉很鄙视摇滚生活,那些整天谈音乐的人在她看来无聊之极。

1974年2月,迪伦与哥伦比亚唱片公司主管、24岁的艾伦·伯恩斯坦(Ellen Bernstein)建立了恋爱关系。春天,迪伦在纽约跟诺曼·雷本(Norman Raeben)学画画。雷本改变了他对时间的理解:"(雷本)教会我如何去观察,他教给了我一种能让我有意识地去做以前我无意识地做事的方式……当我开始这么做时,我制作的第1张专辑就是《轨道上的血》。大家都觉得它是非常不同的,不同之处在于歌词有编码,而且没有时间感;非但如此,它对时间感没有半点尊重。你让昨天、今天和明天共处一室,无法想象其中发生的事少之又少。……我想我只是尝试让它像一幅画,你能看见它的各个部分,又能看到它的整体。"[1]

迪伦自陈,契诃夫短篇小说也在影响他。写这些歌的时候,这位伟大的俄罗斯小说家的身影也在打字机的上空盘旋。

迪伦与艾伦一起在明尼苏达州的农场度过了一段时光,在那里他完成了为这张专辑准备的10首歌曲。克林顿·海林将专辑描述为"也许是20世纪最好的情歌集,充满了触礁的婚姻可以产生的全方位的情感"。

《轨道上的血》证明了,有一种伟大的歌曲,其最强大的力量来自文字,即使脱离了音乐,文字依然感人,仍然可以说它是最优秀的诗篇。然而,这张专辑磅礴的文字、依势而起的音乐、突然发作的歌曲高潮,让最早接触它的音乐家、评论家,都曾产生不同程度的不解。在合作困境中,迪伦放下与摇滚乐队合作的念想,坚定了自我创造、个人原声编曲、自发录音的制作方向。

开篇《忧郁中纠结万端》,实践了迪伦受到绘画启发的歌词写作路线。它从多个层面讲一个故事,情节在空间中叠加,顺序是混乱的,开头可能是结尾。它讲"3个彼此相爱的人,同时陷入了情网"。而"忧郁中纠结万端"这句话是个柱子,稳固地支撑起史诗般庞杂的结构。

《命运的简单戏法》展示了迪伦写小型叙事诗的本事,它是部押韵的小说。在30多行的篇幅内,迪伦精彩讲述

---

[1] Heylin, Clinton (2011). *Behind the Shades: The 20th Anniversary Edition.* Faber & Faber. pp. 368–369.

了一部小说的内容。场景像电影镜头，能在听觉中唤起直观图像，这是歌词不同于诗歌之处。

《你现在是个大女孩了》，我们要为迪伦微妙而又清晰的表达鼓掌。我觉得，把它当成从少女到女人的成长故事来理解最妙。

《愚蠢的风》尤其是一首"想绘成画的歌"，包含了迪伦艺术天分的所有元素。他的无助、他的凄楚、他的怨憎、他的咒骂，最后与他的卑微、他的脆弱、他的深情、他的哀伤融合在一起，成为爱恨交织的极致之作。这首歌显然与迪伦长年受到的舆论重压有关，正是在对重压的反弹中，它喷薄成波澜壮阔、风雷滚滚的呼号之音，涤荡和裹挟着那段时空中的近乎一切。

《愚蠢的风》和《忧郁中纠结万端》的篇幅之长，已足以让我们惊讶，却未料还有《莉莉、罗斯玛丽和红心杰克》。从歌词角度来说，它有恐怖的1400多字（翻译字数）之长；从小说角度来说，它竟能够以1400多字之短，完整、强烈地写出不少于6个人物之间爱恨情仇的故事，可谓神奇。

其他诸作，也都不是等闲之作。《暴风雨中的避难所》有宗教的崇高，呈现了至深的救赎之安抚。《如果你见到她，问声好》，墨水混着昨夜的清泪，结尾处的男性自尊令人莞尔，非常有迪伦的风格……

《轨道上的血》是一张完美的专辑。迪伦回到了20世纪60年代曾连录6张专辑的纽约录音棚，在1974年9月16、17、19、24日和10月8日，录了5场；然后12月27、30日，在明尼阿波利斯录了2场，颠覆了之前录好的5首歌曲。

TANGLED UP IN BLUE

Early one mornin' the sun was shinin'
I was layin' in bed
Wond'rin' if she'd changed at all
If her hair was still red
Her folks they said our lives together
Sure was gonna be rough
They never did like Mama's homemade dress
Papa's bankbook wasn't big enough
And I was standin' on the side of the road
Rain fallin' on my shoes
Heading out for the East Coast
Lord knows I've paid some dues gettin' through
Tangled up in blue

She was married when we first met
Soon to be divorced
I helped her out of a jam, I guess

忧郁中纠结万端 [1]

阳光灿烂的清晨

我躺在床上

寻思她是不是变了

是否她的红发已经变了颜色

她的家人说如果我们走到一起

肯定会很难走

他们向来瞧不上妈妈自制的裙子

爸爸的存折也实在是不厚

所以我站在了路边

任雨水落在鞋面

我动身去了东岸

上帝知道我付出了多少

忧郁中纠结万端

我们第一次见面时她已经嫁人

但是快要离了

我猜是我帮她跳出了坑

---

[1] 迪伦称这首歌用了"十年生活,两年创作"。在现场演唱中,他不时会将歌词中的第一人称换为第三人称。迪伦此时师从诺曼·雷本(1901—1978)学画,改变了认知事物的方式。这首歌不遵循时间顺序,昨天、今天和明天并列,发生的事少之又少,"像一幅画,你能看到不同的部分,又可看到它的整体"。本篇由杨盈盈校译。

But I used a little too much force

We drove that car as far as we could

Abandoned it out West

Split up on a dark sad night

Both agreeing it was best

She turned around to look at me

As I was walkin' away

I heard her say over my shoulder

"We'll meet again someday on the avenue"

Tangled up in blue

I had a job in the great north woods

Working as a cook for a spell

But I never did like it all that much

And one day the ax just fell

So I drifted down to New Orleans

Where I happened to be employed

Workin' for a while on a fishin' boat

Right outside of Delacroix

But all the while I was alone

The past was close behind

I seen a lot of women

But she never escaped my mind, and I just grew

Tangled up in blue

She was workin' in a topless place

但我有些用力过猛
我们尽可能开着那辆车
直到在西部把它扔掉
在漆黑而悲伤的夜里分手
彼此都认为这样最好
这时她转身望着我
我正要迈步离开
就听见她的话从背后传来
"总有一天，我们会在街上重逢"
忧郁中纠结万端

我在北方大森林找工作
当了一段时间大厨
但我从没喜欢过这活儿
直到有一天被解雇
于是我漂到新奥尔良
赶巧被雇用
在渔船上干了一阵儿
就在德拉克洛瓦岛外打工
但自始至终我单身
过去总还跟在身后
我见过许多女人
但是她从未从脑中逃走，我也成熟了
忧郁中纠结万端

她在一个无上装场子打工

And I stopped in for a beer
I just kept lookin' at the side of her face
In the spotlight so clear
And later on as the crowd thinned out
I's just about to do the same
She was standing there in back of my chair
Said to me, "Don't I know your name?"
I muttered somethin' underneath my breath
She studied the lines on my face
I must admit I felt a little uneasy
When she bent down to tie the laces of my shoe
Tangled up in blue

She lit a burner on the stove
And offered me a pipe
"I thought you'd never say hello," she said
"You look like the silent type"
Then she opened up a book of poems
And handed it to me
Written by an Italian poet
From the thirteenth century
And every one of them words rang true
And glowed like burnin' coal
Pourin' off of every page
Like it was written in my soul from me to you
Tangled up in blue

而我停车进去喝杯啤酒
我盯着她的侧影
聚光灯下无比清晰
人群渐去
我也准备走
她走到我椅背后
对我说:"不让我知道你名字吗?"
我小声咕哝了几句
她研读着我脸上的皱纹
必须承认我有点儿不安
当她弯下腰给我系鞋带
忧郁中纠结万端

她点着了火炉
又给我一只烟斗
"我想你不会来打招呼,"她说
"你看似是那种不吭声的类型"
然后她打开一本诗集
将它递给我
是十三世纪
一个意大利诗人的诗
每首诗的语言都很真实
像燃煤一样发着光
从每一页流下来
就像是写在我灵魂里,从我流向你
忧郁中纠结万端

I lived with them on Montague Street
In a basement down the stairs
There was music in the cafés at night
And revolution in the air
Then he started into dealing with slaves
And something inside of him died
She had to sell everything she owned
And froze up inside
And when finally the bottom fell out
I became withdrawn
The only thing I knew how to do
Was to keep on keepin' on like a bird that flew
Tangled up in blue

So now I'm goin' back again
I got to get to her somehow
All the people we used to know
They're an illusion to me now
Some are mathematicians
Some are carpenters' wives
Don't know how it all got started
I don't know what they're doin' with their lives
But me, I'm still on the road
Headin' for another joint
We always did feel the same

我和他们住在蒙塔古街
楼梯下面一个地下室
咖啡馆夜里有音乐
弥漫着革命的气息
他开始与奴隶打交道
内心中的东西死了
她被迫变卖掉家产
将内心冻结
而当最后的底子也掉光
我变得性情孤僻
唯一还晓得怎么去做的
就是像鸟儿一直一直飞
忧郁中纠结万端

所以现在我又回去了
不明所以，我得回她身边去
我们以前认识的人
如今于我都成了幻觉
有的是数学家
有的是木匠妻子
我不明白这一切由何而起
不明白他们怎样过活
只是我，仍在路上
仍在前往下一个歇脚处
我们总有着相同的感受

We just saw it from a different point of view

Tangled up in blue

不同的只是看问题的角度
忧郁中纠结万端

SIMPLE TWIST OF FATE

They sat together in the park
As the evening sky grew dark
She looked at him and he felt a spark tingle to his bones
'Twas then he felt alone and wished that he'd gone straight
And watched out for a simple twist of fate

They walked along by the old canal
A little confused, I remember well
And stopped into a strange hotel with a neon burnin' bright
He felt the heat of the night hit him like a freight train
Moving with a simple twist of fate

A saxophone someplace far off played
As she was walkin' by the arcade
As the light bust through a beat-up shade where he was wakin' up
She dropped a coin into the cup of a blind man at the gate
And forgot about a simple twist of fate

命运的简单戏法 [1]

他们一起坐在公园
当暮色渐渐转暗
她望着他,他感到一束火花刺了他一下
那一刻他感到了孤独,想:一直走下去就好了
并且提防着,命运的简单戏法

他们沿着古运河,走着
有一点儿迷惑,我记得很清楚
他们住进一家陌生旅馆,旅馆上有霓虹闪耀
他感到夜的酷热袭来,像一列货车
呼啸着,命运的简单戏法

一支萨克斯风在很远的地方吹着
而她在街道的拱廊走着
阳光穿过破窗帘,窗帘后他刚
　醒来
她往门口盲人的杯盏里丢了枚硬币
就忘记了,命运的简单戏法

---

[1] 中文有个词叫"造化弄人",本篇题目"Simple Twist of Fate"差不多就是这个意思,本篇由郝佳校译。

He woke up, the room was bare
He didn't see her anywhere
He told himself he didn't care, pushed the window open wide
Felt an emptiness inside to which he just could not relate
Brought on by a simple twist of fate

He hears the ticking of the clocks
And walks along with a parrot that talks
Hunts her down by the waterfront docks where the sailors all come in
Maybe she'll pick him out again, how long must he wait
Once more for a simple twist of fate

People tell me it's a sin
To know and feel too much within
I still believe she was my twin, but I lost the ring
She was born in spring, but I was born too late
Blame it on a simple twist of fate

他醒来,房间里空空如也
四处望去,不见她的身影
他对自己说他不在乎,然后把窗子大开
这时感到内心里有一种说不出来的空虚
带来它的,是命运的简单戏法

他听见钟的嘀嗒
一只说话的鹦鹉陪伴着他
去滨水码头将她追堵,所有的水手都从那儿
　登岸
兴许她还会选上他,他还要再等多久
再一次因为:命运的简单戏法

人们对我说,过分挖掘内心的感受
那也是一种罪
我依然相信她和我天生一对,可是我弄丢了指环
她出生在春天,而我生得太晚
把这一切归咎于:命运的简单戏法

YOU'RE A BIG GIRL NOW

Our conversation was short and sweet
It nearly swept me off-a my feet
And I'm back in the rain, oh, oh
And you are on dry land
You made it there somehow
You're a big girl now

Bird on the horizon, sittin' on a fence
He's singin' his song for me at his own expense
And I'm just like that bird, oh, oh
Singin' just for you
I hope that you can hear
Hear me singin' through these tears

Time is a jet plane, it moves too fast
Oh, but what a shame if all we've shared can't last
I can change, I swear, oh, oh
See what you can do
I can make it through
You can make it too

你现在是个大女孩了 [1]

我们的交谈简短甜美
几乎让我飘了起来
而我回到了雨中,啊,啊
但你在干蓬蓬的地面
真不知你是怎么做到的
你现在是个大女孩了

地平线上的鸟,坐在栅栏上
自费为我唱它的歌
我就像是那只鸟,啊,啊
只为你而唱着
多希望你能听见
听见我饱含泪水的表演

时间是架喷气机,飞得太疾
啊,多可惜,如果我们共度的一切不能继续
我可以改,我发誓,啊,啊
看看你可以做什么
我能扛过去
你也能扛过去

---

[1] 本篇由杨盈盈校译。

Love is so simple, to quote a phrase
You've known it all the time, I'm learnin' it these days
Oh, I know where I can find you, oh, oh
In somebody's room
It's a price I have to pay
You're a big girl all the way

A change in the weather is known to be extreme
But what's the sense of changing horses in midstream?
I'm going out of my mind, oh, oh
With a pain that stops and starts
Like a corkscrew to my heart
Ever since we've been apart

爱如此简单，如某句话所言
对此你一向明白，我是近日才懂得
啊，我知道在哪儿能找到你，啊，啊
在那个人的房间里
这是我必须付出的代价
你完全是个大女孩了

都知道天气变化极端
但在河流中间换马，是什么意思？
我快要疯了，啊，啊
一片剧痛忽停忽始
像有支开瓶螺丝锥在钻我的心
自从我们分手之后

IDIOT WIND

Someone's got it in for me, they're planting stories in the press
Whoever it is I wish they'd cut it out but when they will I can only guess
They say I shot a man named Gray and took his wife to Italy
She inherited a million bucks and when she died it came to me
I can't help it if I'm lucky

People see me all the time and they just can't remember how to act
Their minds are filled with big ideas, images and distorted facts
Even you, yesterday you had to ask me where it was at
I couldn't believe after all these years, you didn't know me better than that
Sweet lady

Idiot wind, blowing every time you move your mouth
Blowing down the backroads headin' south
Idiot wind, blowing every time you move your teeth
You're an idiot, babe
It's a wonder that you still know how to breathe

愚蠢的风 [1]

有人找我的碴儿,在报上编我的故事
不管是谁我希望他收手,但何时收手我也只能
　猜猜
他们说我枪杀了个叫格雷的人,带他老婆去了意大利
她继承了一百万美元,死后钱都归了我
如果我运气这么好那我也没辙

人们每时每刻都看到我,于是忘了该
　怎么做
脑子里塞满了大概念、各种形象和扭曲的事实
就连你,昨天也忍不住问我钱在哪儿
我无法相信这么多年后,你对我的了解不过
　如此
亲爱的女士

愚蠢的风,你嘴一动它就刮起来
沿着小路朝南猛吹
愚蠢的风,你一启齿它就刮起来
你是个白痴,宝贝
你还知道怎么呼吸,真是个奇迹

---

[1] 本篇由杨盈盈校译。

I ran into the fortune-teller, who said beware of lightning that might strike
I haven't known peace and quiet for so long I can't remember what it's like
There's a lone soldier on the cross, smoke pourin' out of a boxcar door
You didn't know it, you didn't think it could be done, in the final end he won the wars
After losin' every battle

I woke up on the roadside, daydreamin' 'bout the way things sometimes are
Visions of your chestnut mare shoot through my head and are makin' me see stars
You hurt the ones that I love best and cover up the truth with lies
One day you'll be in the ditch, flies buzzin' around your eyes
Blood on your saddle

Idiot wind, blowing through the flowers on your tomb
Blowing through the curtains in your room
Idiot wind, blowing every time you move your teeth
You're an idiot, babe
It's a wonder that you still know how to breathe

我碰到那算命的，叫我小心
   遭雷劈
我已太久不得安宁，忘了那是什么
   滋味
十字架上有一个孤独战士，浓烟喷涌出
   货车门
你搞不懂，你觉得不可能，他最后赢了
   战争
尽管输掉了每一场战役

醒来时我在马路边，白日做梦"事情有时就是
   这样"
你栗色母马的幻影击穿了我的头，让我眼冒
   金星
你伤害了我最爱的人，还用谎言掩盖
   真相
总有一天你会栽沟里，苍蝇围着你眼睛嗡嗡嗡
鞍鞯上都是血迹

愚蠢的风，掠过你墓地上的花
掠过你房间的窗帘
愚蠢的风，你一启齿它就刮起来
你是个白痴，宝贝
你还知道怎么呼吸，真是个奇迹

It was gravity which pulled us down and destiny which broke
  us apart
You tamed the lion in my cage but it just wasn't enough to
  change my heart
Now everything's a little upside down, as a matter of fact the
  wheels have stopped
What's good is bad, what's bad is good, you'll find out when
  you reach the top
You're on the bottom

I noticed at the ceremony, your corrupt ways had finally made
  you blind
I can't remember your face anymore, your mouth has changed,
  your eyes don't look into mine
The priest wore black on the seventh day and sat stone-faced
  while the building burned
I waited for you on the running boards, near the cypress trees,
  while the springtime turned
Slowly into autumn

Idiot wind, blowing like a circle around my skull
From the Grand Coulee Dam to the Capitol
Idiot wind, blowing every time you move your teeth
You're an idiot, babe

是重力把我们往下拖,命运将我们
　　分离
你驯服了我笼中的狮子,但还不足以叫我改变
　　心意
如今一切都有些颠倒,事实上巨轮已经
　　停下
好成了坏,坏成了好,等到了顶点你就
　　知道了
你正在谷底

典礼上我注意到,你的堕落最后让你
　　视而不见
我记不起你的脸了,你的嘴变了,
　　你不再直视我双眼
在第七天,牧师一身漆黑板脸坐着,
　　大厦在燃烧
我在车踏板上等你,旁边是柏树,
　　此时春天缓慢地
变成了秋天

愚蠢的风,像一个环围着我头骨吹
从大古力水坝[1]吹到国会大厦
愚蠢的风,你一启齿它就刮起来
你是个白痴,宝贝

---

[1] 大古力水坝,美国最大的水利电力水坝,在华盛顿州哥伦比亚河上。

It's a wonder that you still know how to breathe

I can't feel you anymore, I can't even touch
   the books you've read
Every time I crawl past your door, I been wishin' I was
   somebody else instead
Down the highway, down the tracks, down the road to ecstasy
I followed you beneath the stars, hounded by your memory
And all your ragin' glory

I been double-crossed now for the very last time and now I'm
   finally free
I kissed goodbye the howling beast on the borderline which
   separated you from me
You'll never know the hurt I suffered nor the pain I rise above
And I'll never know the same about you, your holiness or your
   kind of love
And it makes me feel so sorry

Idiot wind, blowing through the buttons of our coats
Blowing through the letters that we wrote
Idiot wind, blowing through the dust upon our shelves
We're idiots, babe
It's a wonder we can even feed ourselves

你还知道怎么呼吸，真是个奇迹

我再也无法感觉你，甚至不能碰
　　你读过的书
每次缓缓走过你门前，我都希望
　　我是别人
沿着公路，沿着铁轨，沿着心驰神往之途
我在星空下跟随你，被你的记忆
和你所有怒放的荣光，紧紧追逐

这是我最后一次被出卖，现在我终获
　　自由
在分开了你我的界线上，我吻别了那只
　　嚎叫的野兽
你永远不会懂我承受的伤和我克服的痛
我也同样永远不会懂你，懂你的圣洁和你的
　　那种爱
这让我深感遗憾

愚蠢的风，吹过我们外套上的纽扣
吹过我们往来的一封封信
愚蠢的风，吹我们架子上的灰
我们是白痴，宝贝
我们还可以养活自己，真是个奇迹

YOU'RE GONNA MAKE ME LONESOME WHEN YOU GO

I've seen love go by my door

It's never been this close before

Never been so easy or so slow

Been shooting in the dark too long

When somethin's not right it's wrong

Yer gonna make me lonesome when you go

Dragon clouds so high above

I've only known careless love

It's always hit me from below

This time around it's more correct

Right on target, so direct

Yer gonna make me lonesome when you go

Purple clover, Queen Anne's lace

Crimson hair across your face

You could make me cry if you don't know

Can't remember what I was thinkin' of

你走了会让我寂寞 [1]

我看见爱从门前经过
从未曾这么近
从未曾这么缓慢和从容
在黑暗中穿行太久
若有事不对那就是错的
你走了会让我寂寞

龙云如此高高在上
我只熟知无心之爱
总会从下方击中我
这一次它更准
正中靶心,这么直接
你走了会让我寂寞

紫色三叶草,安妮女王的花边 [2]
深红色头发遮住你的脸
是否你不知道,你会使我哭泣
让我都不记得我刚才想的

---

[1] 本篇由杨盈盈校译。
[2] 安妮女王的花边,一种野胡萝卜的别称。

You might be spoilin' me too much, love
Yer gonna make me lonesome when you go

Flowers on the hillside, bloomin' crazy
Crickets talkin' back and forth in rhyme
Blue river runnin' slow and lazy
I could stay with you forever and never realize the time

Situations have ended sad
Relationships have all been bad
Mine've been like Verlaine's and Rimbaud
But there's no way I can compare
All those scenes to this affair
Yer gonna make me lonesome when you go

Yer gonna make me wonder what I'm doin'
Stayin' far behind without you
Yer gonna make me wonder what I'm sayin'
Yer gonna make me give myself a good talkin' to

I'll look for you in old Honolulu
San Francisco, Ashtabula

你可能宠坏了我,亲爱的
你走了会让我寂寞

山坡上的花,疯狂开放
蟋蟀们押着韵反复交谈
蓝色的河缓慢而慵懒地流淌
我可以永远陪伴你而忘记了时间

所有的状况都已可悲地终结
所有的关系都已经崩坏
我的处境就像魏尔伦和兰波 [1]
但我无法拿那些场景
比较这次的恋情
你走了会让我寂寞

你会让我奇怪我在做什么
远远地落在后面,不见你的踪影
你会让我奇怪我在说什么
你会让我跟我自己狠狠地说一通

我会去老檀香山找你
去旧金山,去阿什塔比拉 [2]

---

[1] 魏尔伦和兰波,19世纪的两位传奇法国诗人,魏尔伦迷恋兰波,一度为他放弃妻小一起流亡英国。
[2] 檀香山、旧金山、阿什塔比拉,均为美国地名。

Yer gonna have to leave me now, I know
But I'll see you in the sky above
In the tall grass, in the ones I love
Yer gonna make me lonesome when you go

你现在必须离开我,我知道
但我会见到你,在头顶的天空中
在高高的草丛中,在我所爱的人中
你走了会让我寂寞

MEET ME IN THE MORNING

Meet me in the morning, 56th and Wabasha
Meet me in the morning, 56th and Wabasha
Honey, we could be in Kansas
By time the snow begins to thaw

They say the darkest hour is right before the dawn
They say the darkest hour is right before the dawn
But you wouldn't know it by me
Every day's been darkness since you been gone

Little rooster crowin', there must be something on his mind
Little rooster crowin', there must be something on his mind
Well, I feel just like that rooster
Honey, ya treat me so unkind

The birds are flyin' low babe, honey I feel so exposed
Well, the birds are flyin' low babe, honey I feel so exposed
Well now, I ain't got any matches
And the station doors are closed

早上来见我

早上来见我,在 56 街和瓦巴肖 [1]
早上来见我,在 56 街和瓦巴肖
亲爱的,我们可以去堪萨斯
当积雪开始融化

他们说最黑暗的时刻就在黎明前
他们说最黑暗的时刻就在黎明前
然而你不会从我这儿知晓
自你离开后,每一天都很黑暗

小公鸡在啼鸣,他一定有什么心事
小公鸡在啼鸣,他一定有什么心事
唉,我感觉我就像是那只公鸡
亲爱的,你对我实在不友善

鸟飞得很低宝贝,亲爱的我感到我无遮无拦
唉,鸟飞得很低宝贝,亲爱的我感到我无遮无拦
唉现在,我没有任何人结伴
车站的门也关了

---

[1] 瓦巴肖,美国地名,在明尼苏达州。

Well, I struggled through barbed wire, felt the hail fall from
 above
Well, I struggled through barbed wire, felt the hail fall from
 above
Well, you know I even outran the hound dogs
Honey, you know I've earned your love

Look at the sun sinkin' like a ship
Look at the sun sinkin' like a ship
Ain't that just like my heart, babe
When you kissed my lips?

唉,我挣扎着穿过铁丝网,感觉到冰雹兜头
　砸下
唉,我挣扎着穿过铁丝网,感觉到冰雹兜头
　砸下
唉,你知道我跑得比猎犬还快
亲爱的,你知道我赢过你的爱

看太阳像一艘船下沉
看太阳像一艘船下沉
可不就像是我的心,宝贝
当你吻过了我的嘴唇?

LILY, ROSEMARY AND THE JACK OF HEARTS

The festival was over, the boys were all plannin' for a fall
The cabaret was quiet except for the drillin' in the wall
The curfew had been lifted and the gamblin' wheel shut down
Anyone with any sense had already left town
He was standin' in the doorway lookin' like the Jack of Hearts

He moved across the mirrored room, "Set it up for everyone," he said
Then everyone commenced to do what they were doin' before he turned their heads
Then he walked up to a stranger and he asked him with a grin
"Could you kindly tell me, friend, what time the show begins?"
Then he moved into the corner, face down like the Jack of Hearts

Backstage the girls were playin' five-card stud by the stairs
Lily had two queens, she was hopin' for a third to match her pair

莉莉、罗斯玛丽和红心杰克 [1]

节日结束了,小伙子们都在为秋天做打算
卡巴莱舞厅安静下来,除了墙上的电钻
宵禁已解除,轮盘赌已关停
有理智的人都离开了小城
他站在门口,看起来就像红心杰克

他穿过镜子大厅。"给每个人都预备好了,"
  他说
大家把头转向他,然后继续
  手头在做的事
然后他走到一个陌生人面前,笑着问他
"朋友,请问演出几点开始?"
然后他走进角落,面朝下,
  就像红心杰克

后台的女孩子在楼梯旁玩五张梭哈 [2]
莉莉有两张王后,她希望来第三张配她的
  对子

---

[1] 本篇中有不少关于扑克牌面的隐语。如王后、国王以及红心杰克。
[2] 梭哈(Show Hand),学名五张种马(Five Card Stud),是扑克游戏的一种。以五张牌的排列组合、点数和花色大小决定胜负。

Outside the streets were fillin' up, the window was open wide
A gentle breeze was blowin', you could feel it from inside
Lily called another bet and drew up the Jack of Hearts

Big Jim was no one's fool, he owned the town's only diamond mine
He made his usual entrance lookin' so dandy and so fine
With his bodyguards and silver cane and every hair in place
He took whatever he wanted to and he laid it all to waste
But his bodyguards and silver cane were no match for the Jack of Hearts

Rosemary combed her hair and took a carriage into town
She slipped in through the side door lookin' like a queen without a crown
She fluttered her false eyelashes and whispered in his ear
"Sorry, darlin', that I'm late," but he didn't seem to hear
He was starin' into space over at the Jack of Hearts

"I know I've seen that face before," Big Jim was thinkin' to himself
"Maybe down in Mexico or a picture up on somebody's shelf"
But then the crowd began to stamp their feet and the houselights did dim
And in the darkness of the room there was only Jim and him
Starin' at the butterfly who just drew the Jack of Hearts

外面街道正汹涌,窗户大开
一阵微风吹过,你从里面都能感觉到
莉莉又叫了次注,上手了红心杰克

大个儿吉姆可不是傻瓜,他拥有城里唯一的
　钻石矿
每次出场总是讲究而时髦
带着保镖,拈着银手杖,头发一丝不苟
他想要什么就要什么,然后把它们全浪费掉
但他的保镖和银手杖,都敌不过
　红心杰克

罗斯玛丽梳好了头,坐着马车进城
她从侧门翩然而入,看起来像是无冕的
　王后
抖动着假睫毛,她在他耳畔低语
"对不起,亲爱的,我来晚了,"但他似乎没听到
穿过眼前的空白瞪着红心杰克

"这张脸我以前肯定见过,"大个儿吉姆
　心想
"也许在墨西哥,或是谁书架的照片上"
但随后人群开始跺脚,室灯
　暗了
而在房间的黑暗里只有吉姆和他
凝视着那只蝴蝶,她刚上手了红心杰克

Lily was a princess, she was fair-skinned and precious as a child
She did whatever she had to do, she had that certain flash every time she smiled
She'd come away from a broken home, had lots of strange affairs
With men in every walk of life which took her everywhere
But she'd never met anyone quite like the Jack of Hearts

The hangin' judge came in unnoticed and was being wined and dined
The drillin' in the wall kept up but no one seemed to pay it any mind
It was known all around that Lily had Jim's ring
And nothing would ever come between Lily and the king
No, nothin' ever would except maybe the Jack of Hearts

Rosemary started drinkin' hard and seein' her reflection in the knife
She was tired of the attention, tired of playin' the role of Big Jim's wife
She had done a lot of bad things, even once tried suicide
Was lookin' to do just one good deed before she died
She was gazin' to the future, riding on the Jack of Hearts

莉莉是个公主,白净精致面如
　　孩童
她做她必须做的事,每次微笑都有一丝
　　光芒闪过
她从破碎的家逃出来,有过许多
　　风流韵事
三教九流的男人带她出入各种场合
但她从未见过哪个人像红心杰克

绞刑官悄悄进来了,正在喝酒
　　吃饭
墙上的电钻一直响,但似乎没谁
　　听见
周围人都知道莉莉有吉姆的戒指
而莉莉和国王之间永远不会有事
是的,不会有任何事,也许除了红心杰克

罗斯玛丽开始大口喝酒,在餐刀上看到她的
　　影子
她厌倦了受关注,厌倦了扮演大个儿吉姆的
　　妻子
她干过许多糟心事,甚至还自杀过一次
在死前她只想做件好事
她盯着那未来,寄望于红心杰克

Lily washed her face, took her dress off and buried it away
"Has your luck run out?" she laughed at him, "Well, I guess
 you must have known it would someday
Be careful not to touch the wall, there's a brand-new coat of
 paint
I'm glad to see you're still alive, you're lookin' like a saint"
Down the hallway footsteps were comin' for the Jack of Hearts

The backstage manager was pacing all around by his chair
"There's something funny going on," he said, "I can just feel it
 in the air"
He went to get the hangin' judge, but the hangin' judge was
 drunk
As the leading actor hurried by in the costume of a monk
There was no actor anywhere better than the Jack of Hearts

Lily's arms were locked around the man that she dearly loved
 to touch
She forgot all about the man she couldn't stand who hounded
 her so much
"I've missed you so," she said to him, and he felt she was
 sincere
But just beyond the door he felt jealousy and fear
Just another night in the life of the Jack of Hearts

No one knew the circumstance but they say that it happened

莉莉洗了脸,脱下裙子,把它藏起来
"你的运气用完了?"她笑他,"嗯,我猜
 你准知道会有今日
小心别碰墙,才漆了
 新漆
真高兴见你还活着,看上去像个圣徒"
脚步声沿着走廊,在走向红心杰克

后台经理围着椅子在踱步
"有些怪事发生,"他说,"我能在空气中
 感觉到"
他去找绞刑官,但绞刑官
 醉了
当男主角身穿僧侣服匆匆而过
没有更好的演员了,会比得过红心杰克

莉莉用双臂环绕着她深爱的
 情人
完全忘记了那个她无法忍受的、甩不掉的
 男人
"我好想你,"她对他说,他觉得她
 情真意切
但就在一门之外,让他感到嫉妒和恐惧
这不过是生命中的又一夜,属于红心杰克

没人知道当时的情况,但据说事情发生得

97

pretty quick
The door to the dressing room burst open and a cold revolver clicked
And Big Jim was standin' there, ya couldn't say surprised
Rosemary right beside him, steady in her eyes
She was with Big Jim but she was leanin' to the Jack of Hearts

Two doors down the boys finally made it through the wall
And cleaned out the bank safe, it's said that they got off with quite a haul
In the darkness by the riverbed they waited on the ground
For one more member who had business back in town
But they couldn't go no further without the Jack of Hearts

The next day was hangin' day, the sky was overcast and black
Big Jim lay covered up, killed by a penknife in the back
And Rosemary on the gallows, she didn't even blink
The hangin' judge was sober, he hadn't had a drink
The only person on the scene missin' was the Jack of Hearts

The cabaret was empty now, a sign said, "Closed for repair"
Lily had already taken all of the dye out of her hair
She was thinkin' 'bout her father, who she very rarely saw
Thinkin' 'bout Rosemary and thinkin' about the law
But most of all she was thinkin' 'bout the Jack of Hearts

很快
更衣室的门突然开了,一把冰冷的左轮枪
　　咔嗒一响
大个儿吉姆站那儿,你不能说没想到
罗斯玛丽就在他身边,眼神坚定
她跟着大个儿吉姆,但她倾向了红心杰克

干倒了两重门,小伙子们破墙而入
洗劫了银行保险柜,据说搞了
　　一大笔
在河床边的黑暗中,他们在空地上等着
一个同伙回城里有事要办
而他们走不远,如果没有红心杰克

第二天是绞刑日,天空乌云密布
大个儿吉姆躺着,盖着布,被把小折刀从背后杀死
而罗斯玛丽上了绞架,她眼睛都没眨
绞刑官很清醒,他没喝酒
现场唯一失踪的人,是红心杰克

如今卡巴莱舞厅空空如也,牌子上写着:"停业维修"
莉莉洗去了头发上所有的染色剂
她在想她很少见到的父亲
想着罗斯玛丽,想着法律
但想得最多的,是红心杰克

IF YOU SEE HER SAY HELLO

If you see her, say hello, she might be in Tangier
It's the city 'cross the water, not too far from here
Say for me that I'm all right though things are kind of slow
She might think that I've forgotten her. Don't tell her it isn't so

We had a falling-out, like lovers sometimes do
But to think of how she left that night, it hurts me through and through
And though our situation pierced me to the bone
I got to find someone to take her place. I don't like to be alone

I see a lot of people as I make the rounds
And I hear her name here and there as I go from town to town
And I've never gotten used to it, I've just learned to turn it off
Her eyes were blue, her hair was too, her skin so sweet and soft

Sundown, yellow moon, I replay the past

如果你见到她，问声好 [1]

如果你见到她，问声好，她可能在丹吉尔 [2]
隔水相望就是那座城，离这儿不很远
跟她说我都好，虽然进展有点慢
或许她以为我忘了她。别告诉她这并非实情

我们闹翻了，恋人们有时就这样
可想想那晚她离开的情形，真让我
  伤透心
尽管我们的情深入我骨髓
我还是必须找人顶她。我不想孤独一人

我四方游走，见过不少人
一城一城，这里那里，到处听到她的芳名
这让我实在不习惯，我只好学会不听
她的眼睛是蓝的，头发也是蓝的，她的皮肤芬芳而柔软

日落，黄月亮，我回放着过去

---

[1] 本篇由杨盈盈校译。
[2] 丹吉尔，摩洛哥北部港口城市。听众一般会假定故事发生在美国，但实际上丹吉尔与美国隔着一个大西洋，所以"隔水相望就是那座城，离这儿不很远"是个幽默。

I know every scene by heart, they all went by so fast
If she's passin' back this way, and I sure hope she don't
Tell her she can look me up. I'll either be here or I won't

我心知那每一幕，它们都去得好快
假如她再走回这条路，但愿她不会
跟她说可以来看看我啊。我可能在这儿可能不在

SHELTER FROM THE STORM

'Twas in another lifetime, one of toil and blood
When blackness was a virtue and the road was full of mud
I came in from the wilderness, a creature void of form
"Come in," she said, "I'll give you shelter from the storm"

And if I pass this way again, you can rest assured
I'll always do my best for her, on that I give my word
In a world of steel-eyed death, and men who are fighting to be warm
"Come in," she said, "I'll give you shelter from the storm"

Not a word was spoke between us, there was little risk involved
Everything up to that point had been left unresolved
Try imagining a place where it's always safe and warm
"Come in," she said, "I'll give you shelter from the storm"

I was burned out from exhaustion, buried in the hail
Poisoned in the bushes an' blown out on the trail
Hunted like a crocodile, ravaged in the corn
"Come in," she said, "I'll give you shelter from the storm"

Suddenly I turned around and she was standin' there

暴风雨中的避难所

是在另一回生命中,那一生都是辛劳和血
邪恶是美德,而道路上尽是烂泥
我从荒野走来,是一个没了形的造物
"进来吧,"她说,"我给你暴风雨中的避难所"

设若我能重来一次,你放心
我会始终为她全力以赴,对此我保证
在一个被死亡盯牢的世界,人们为一点温暖而
　　拼争
"进来吧,"她说,"我给你暴风雨中的避难所"

我们之间未置一词,几乎不涉危险
在那一刻到来之前,一切都悬而未决
试着想象一个地方,永远安全而温暖
"进来吧,"她说,"我给你暴风雨中的避难所"

我耗尽力气油尽灯枯,被冰雹埋葬
在灌木丛里中毒,在小路上被吹熄
像鳄鱼一样被猎杀,蹂躏于玉米地
"进来吧,"她说,"我给你暴风雨中的避难所"

突然我转过身,而她就站在那里

With silver bracelets on her wrists and flowers in her hair
She walked up to me so gracefully and took my crown of
   thorns
"Come in," she said, "I'll give you shelter from the storm"

Now there's a wall between us, somethin' there's been lost
I took too much for granted, got my signals crossed
Just to think that it all began on a long-forgotten morn
"Come in," she said, "I'll give you shelter from the storm"

Well, the deputy walks on hard nails and the preacher rides a
   mount
But nothing really matters much, it's doom alone that counts
And the one-eyed undertaker, he blows a futile horn
"Come in," she said, "I'll give you shelter from the storm"

I've heard newborn babies wailin' like a mournin' dove
And old men with broken teeth stranded without love
Do I understand your question, man, is it hopeless and forlorn?
"Come in," she said, "I'll give you shelter from the storm"

In a little hilltop village, they gambled for my clothes
I bargained for salvation an' they gave me a lethal dose
I offered up my innocence and got repaid with scorn
"Come in," she said, "I'll give you shelter from the storm"

手腕上戴着银手镯,头发上簪着花朵
她如此优雅走向我,取下我的
 荆冠
"进来吧,"她说,"我给你暴风雨中的避难所"

如今一堵墙立在我们之间,有些东西遗失了
我太过想当然,叉掉了我的信号
只觉得这一切都始于一个早已遗忘的清晨
"进来吧,"她说,"我给你暴风雨中的避难所"

唉,代理人走在钉尖,传教士
 骑着马
但没什么事真的重要,唯一算数的只有死亡
那独眼的殡仪员吹着一只无用的号角
"进来吧,"她说,"我给你暴风雨中的避难所"

我听见新生儿号哭像只哀鸽
而断齿的老人们在无爱中搁浅
我明白你的问题吗,老兄,是不是无望又孤立无助?
"进来吧,"她说,"我给你暴风雨中的避难所"

在一个山顶小村庄,他们赌我的衣裳
我为救赎讨价还价,他们却给了我致命的剂量
我献出我的清白,换回的却是轻蔑
"进来吧,"她说,"我给你暴风雨中的避难所"

Well, I'm livin' in a foreign country but I'm bound to cross the line

Beauty walks a razor's edge, someday I'll make it mine

If I could only turn back the clock to when God and her were born

"Come in," she said, "I'll give you shelter from the storm"

唉,我生活在异邦但我注定要
　越界
美在刀锋上行走,有朝一日我要它属于我
如果我能把时钟拨回上帝和她诞生的
　一刻
"进来吧,"她说,"我给你暴风雨中的避难所"

BUCKETS OF RAIN

Buckets of rain
Buckets of tears
Got all them buckets comin' out of my ears
Buckets of moonbeams in my hand
I got all the love, honey baby
You can stand

I been meek
And hard like an oak
I seen pretty people disappear like smoke
Friends will arrive, friends will disappear
If you want me, honey baby
I'll be here

Like your smile
And your fingertips
Like the way that you move your lips
I like the cool way you look at me
Everything about you is bringing me
Misery

Little red wagon

倾盆的雨

倾盆的雨
倾盆的泪
这全部的倾盆之物自我双耳涌出
倾盆的月光在我手心里
我拥有这全部的爱,亲爱的
你能承受住

我一直逆来顺受
又强硬得像棵橡树
眼见着漂亮人儿轻烟一样消失
朋友们来的来,朋友们去的去
如果你要我,亲爱的
我就在这里

喜欢你的笑
还有你的指尖
喜欢你轻启嘴唇的样子
我喜欢你看我时的冷漠
你的一切都让我
难过

可爱的红马车

Little red bike
I ain't no monkey but I know what I like
I like the way you love me strong and slow
I'm takin' you with me, honey baby
When I go

Life is sad
Life is a bust
All ya can do is do what you must
You do what you must do and ya do it well
I'll do it for you, honey baby
Can't you tell?

可爱的红单车
我没有胡闹,我知道我喜欢什么
我喜欢你那样坚定又缓慢地爱我
我要带你走,亲爱的
当我离去时

人生悲哀
人生是场失败
你所能做的就是做你必须做的
你做你必须做的,并且做好
我也会为你这样,亲爱的
难道你不明白?

UP TO ME

Everything went from bad to worse, money never changed a thing
Death kept followin', trackin' us down, at least I heard your bluebird sing
Now somebody's got to show their hand, time is an enemy
I know you're long gone, I guess it must be up to me

If I'd thought about it I never would've done it, I guess I would've let it slide
If I'd lived my life by what others were thinkin', the heart inside me would've died
I was just too stubborn to ever be governed by enforced insanity
Someone had to reach for the risin' star, I guess it was up to me

Oh, the Union Central is pullin' out and the orchids are in bloom
I've only got me one good shirt left and it smells of stale perfume

得我来 [1]

一切都变得更糟，金钱从来
   改变不了
死亡一直尾随身后，至少我听到你的
   蓝鸟在叫
现在得有人亮底牌了，时间是敌人
我知道你早已离去，我想这事得我来搞

这事如果早想过，我就绝不会这么做，我想我会
   任由它去
如果我按别人的想法过活，我的心早就已经
   完结
我只是太倔强，从未被强迫性的精神错乱
   制服
得有人伸手摘取那升起的星，我想这事得我来做

啊，"联合中央" [2] 在撤出，兰花
   正在开
我只剩最后一件好衬衣，闻着有一股陈旧的
   香气

---

[1] 本篇由杨盈盈校译。
[2] 联合中央，美国人寿保险公司，于 1867 年创立，2013 年被兼并。

In fourteen months I've only smiled once and I didn't do it consciously
Somebody's got to find your trail, I guess it must be up to me

It was like a revelation when you betrayed me with your touch
I'd just about convinced myself that nothin' had changed that much
The old Rounder in the iron mask slipped me the master key
Somebody had to unlock your heart, he said it was up to me

Well, I watched you slowly disappear down into the officers' club
I would've followed you in the door but I didn't have a ticket stub
So I waited all night 'til the break of day, hopin' one of us could get free
When the dawn came over the river bridge, I knew it was up to me

Oh, the only decent thing I did when I worked as a postal clerk
Was to haul your picture down off the wall near the cage where I used to work
Was I a fool or not to try to protect your identity?
You looked a little burned out, my friend, I thought it might be up to me

十四个月我只笑过一次,并且我根本
　　没意识到
必须有人找到你的踪迹,我想这事得我来搞

这就像是个启示,当你以你的方式背叛我
我眼看着要说服自己:一切并没改变
　　太多
戴铁面罩的老惯犯塞给我万能钥匙
总得有人开启你的心,他说这事得我来做

好吧,我看着你慢慢消失,潜入军官
　　俱乐部
我本来要跟你进去,可是我没有通行
　　票据
于是我守了一夜直到天亮,希望我们俩
　　有一人能逃离
当黎明从跨河大桥掠过,我知道这事得
　　我来操持

啊,我当邮政员时唯一做得像样的事
是把你的照片从我工棚旁的墙上
　　撕去
极力要保护你的身份,我是不是傻了?
你看上去有点精疲力竭,我的朋友,我想
　　这也许该我负责

Well, I met somebody face to face and I had to remove my hat
She's everything I need and love but I can't be swayed by that
It frightens me, the awful truth of how sweet life can be
But she ain't a-gonna make me move, I guess it must be up to me

We heard the Sermon on the Mount and I knew it was too complex
It didn't amount to anything more than what the broken glass reflects
When you bite off more than you can chew you pay the penalty
Somebody's got to tell the tale, I guess it must be up to me

Well, Dupree came in pimpin' tonight to the Thunderbird Café
Crystal wanted to talk to him, I had to look the other way
Well, I just can't rest without you, love, I need your company
But you ain't a-gonna cross the line, I guess it must be up to me

There's a note left in the bottle, you can give it to Estelle
She's the one you been wond'rin' about, but there's really nothin' much to tell
We both heard voices for a while, now the rest is history
Somebody's got to cry some tears, I guess it must be up to me

哦，我曾和某人面对面，还不得不摘下了帽子
她是我需要和深爱的一切，但我不能为此动摇
生活竟能如此甜蜜，这可怕的事实吓坏了我
然而她不会让我搬走，我想这事得靠
　　我自己

我们都听过登山宝训[1]，我知道它实在
　　复杂
但它的意味再多，也多不过碎玻璃的
　　反射
当你贪多嚼不烂时，你就要付出代价
总该有人讲讲这事，我想这必须我来做

唉，杜普雷今晚来雷鸟咖啡馆拉皮条
克里斯特尔想和他说话，我只好眼往别处瞧
唉，没有你我无法安宁，亲爱的，我需要你陪伴
可是你不会越线，我想这事得我来办

瓶子里留了张字条，你可以交给埃丝特尔
她这个人你一直在琢磨，但其实真没什么
　　需要弄清
我们都听到些一时的议论，现在剩下的才是历史
必须有人哭出眼泪，我想这事得我来完成

---

[1] 登山宝训，耶稣基督在山上传道时所说的话。

So go on, boys, and play your hands, life is a pantomime
The ringleaders from the county seat say you don't have all that
    much time
And the girl with me behind the shades, she ain't my property
One of us has got to hit the road, I guess it must be up to me

And if we never meet again, baby, remember me
How my lone guitar played sweet for you that old-time melody
And the harmonica around my neck, I blew it for you, free
No one else could play that tune, you know it was up to me

所以继续吧小伙子们,耍耍你们的手,生活是出哑剧
县城的头头们说,你们已没有多少
　　时间
而阴影后跟着我的那位姑娘,她不是我的财产
我们其中一人必须上路,我想这事得我来承担

假如我们再也不相见,宝贝,记住我
我孤独的吉他是如何为你甜蜜地弹奏那好时光的歌
还有挂在我脖子上的口琴,我为你吹过,免费的
没有人能奏出那种调子,你知道这只有我能做

CALL LETTER BLUES

Well, I walked all night long
Listenin' to them church bells tone
Yes, I walked all night long
Listenin' to them church bells tone
Either someone needing mercy
Or maybe something I've done wrong

Well, your friends come by for you
I don't know what to say
Well, your friends come by for you
I don't know what to say
I just can't face up to tell 'em
Honey you just went away

Well, children cry for mother
I tell them, "Mother took a trip"
Well, children cry for mother
I tell them, "Mother took a trip"
Well, I walk on pins and needles
I hope my tongue don't slip

Well, I gaze at passing strangers

呼号蓝调

唉，我走了一整夜
听着教堂的钟声
是啊，我走了一整夜
听着教堂的钟声
不是有人需要宽恕
就是有些事我可能错了

唉，朋友们来找你
我不知道说什么
唉，朋友们来找你
我不知道说什么
我该怎么当面告诉他们
亲爱的你刚刚走了

唉，孩子们哭着要妈
我告诉他们："妈妈旅行去了"
唉，孩子们哭着要妈
我告诉他们："妈妈旅行去了"
唉，我在针尖上走
但愿我不会说漏嘴

唉，我盯着过路的人

In case I might see you
Yes, I gaze at passing strangers
In case I might see you
But the sun goes around the heavens
And another day just drives on through

万一可能看见你
是啊,我盯着过路的人
万一可能看见你
可太阳围着天空转
又一天过去了

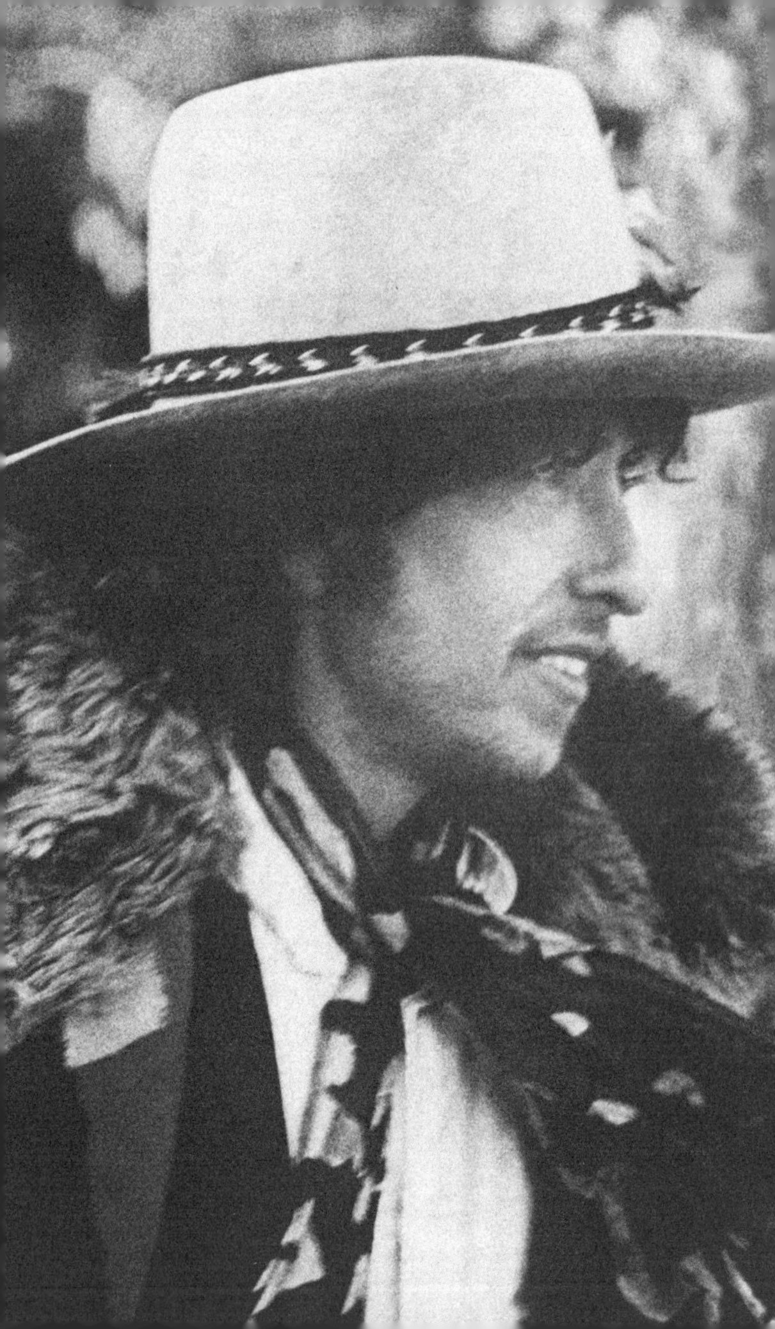

DESIRE
渴望

飓风

伊西丝

莫桑比克

再喝一杯咖啡(下面的溪谷)

哦,姐姐

乔伊

杜兰戈罗曼史

黑钻石湾

萨拉

附加歌词

被遗弃的爱

鲇鱼

金纺车

丽塔·梅

七天

手语

金钱蓝调

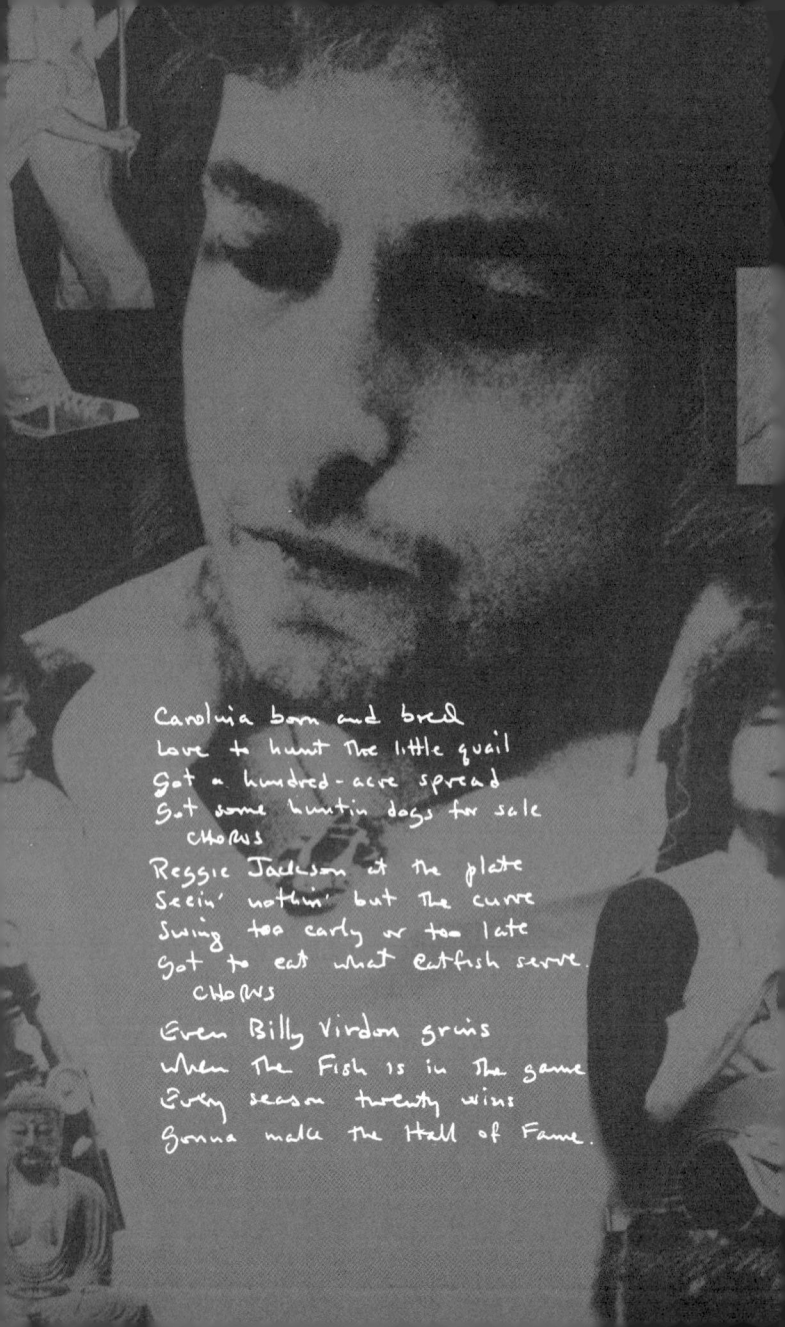

Carolina born and bred
Love to hunt the little quail
Got a hundred-acre spread
Got some huntin dogs for sale
  CHORUS
Reggie Jackson at the plate
Seein' nothin' but the curve
Swing too early or too late
Got to eat what Catfish serve.
  CHORUS
Even Billy Virdon grins
When the Fish is in the game
Every season twenty wins
Gonna make the Hall of Fame.

虽然迪伦一再地令我惊讶,但《渴望》还是让我难以相信,像是遇到了某种违反物理定律的不可能。这张专辑里居然有 5 首属于迪伦的长叙事曲,不知他是怎么装进去的。它们都像小说,《黑钻石湾》还像是长篇小说。这是迪伦的第 17 张录音室专辑,于 1976 年 1 月 5 日由哥伦比亚唱片公司发行。

在这张专辑诞生前,迪伦的创作变得缓慢,我觉得,近乎枯竭。但迪伦此时有了一个转变,他打定了主意,要找人一起写歌词。他找到的人,是作家、剧作家和戏剧总监雅克·利维。与他见面后的第一次深谈,迪伦的写作僵局就被打开了,他与利维在不到 4 个星期内,就写出了专辑中全部的 9 首歌曲。

还有一个变化,对迪伦来说意义同等重大。他一个人搬进了纽约格林尼治村,因此得以见识女诗人帕蒂·史密斯(Patti Smith)和她的乐队,乐队与个人间强烈的化学反应,"那独特的摇滚声音"让他震惊,他决意也要组建自己的创造性的乐队,让他能更即兴地创作并在"语言方面"扩展自己。

迪伦由此找来的乐手,诡异至极。小提琴手斯卡莉特·里韦拉（Scarlet Rivera）是在街上碰到的，迪伦找上她只因为看到她拎着琴盒。配二重唱的女歌手艾米露·哈里斯（Emmylou Harris），迪伦和她互不认识，找上她可能是因为哥伦比亚唱片公司有位监制是她的歌迷。后来的录音证明，她们都发挥了神妙的作用。

但这张专辑刚开始的录音都是灾难。1975年7月14、28和29日，迪伦聚集了临时找来的乐手，进行了3场混乱不堪的录音。人数最多时，现场有20位乐手及和声歌手，埃里克·克莱普顿（Eric Clapton）也在其中，是5位吉他手之一！每个人都深感挫败，队伍一减再减，终于魔法般地缩减到较小规模。在7月30、31日，8月11日，10月24日，队员们每一位都如有神助，配合默契无间。

一个小细节足以说明这是支什么样的队伍，以及这是怎样一种合作方式。据艾米露·哈里斯回忆："我们握了下手，就开始录歌了。我对这些歌一无所知，不过歌词就在面前，乐队开始演奏，他（迪伦）要我唱的时候就戳我一下。我也不知道我是怎么做到的，但我真的是一只眼睛看着他的嘴，一只眼睛看着歌词。"[1]

直到今天，任何一个人都仍然可以在《再喝一杯咖啡（下面的溪谷）》中，听到艾米露那略显生涩，却也是百分百新鲜的配唱。如野梨一般香气四溢，她与迪伦的那种绝佳契合，真是美好而神秘。

每一首歌词都有几分传奇色彩，先看5首长篇。

《飓风》，相当于申冤歌曲。在看过鲁宾·卡特的自传

---

[1] [法] 马戈汀, 古斯登. 鲍勃·迪伦的歌：492首歌背后的故事[M]. 江岭, 孙佳慧, 郁梦非, 等译. 郑州：河南大学出版社, 2019.

并在监狱见他一面之后，迪伦即坚信他是无辜的，是遭人陷害。1985 年，18 年牢狱之苦之后，一位最高法院法官撤销了所有指控，卡特被释放。

《伊西丝》，寓言般的爱情故事。要想知道它有多精彩，只需读读倒数第 2 段。自然、极简又意味深长的神奇对话，竟以这般形式出现在一首歌曲里。而且，这富有象征意义的对话，以极致的简洁，展现了男女主人公的微妙心理和可爱性格。

《杜兰戈罗曼史》，是由生写到死，最后 3 段是将死、正死、已死之人的话，直接呈现了这份情至死不渝。更为感人的是，整首歌如骑在马背上，极为形象地表现了如烈马和烈焰一般对于生命的渴望，对于飞扬人生和自由的追求，堪称美国南部边疆最传奇的荒芜英雄浪漫史。

《黑钻石湾》，谜一般的人物和情节，谜一般的氛围和叙事，这样的宏大和瑰奇，还有哪一首歌曲能做到？而整首诗的架构，有如现代小说，如拓扑般彼此嵌入，透射出后现代主义的冷漠……

再看几首短篇。《再喝一杯咖啡（下面的溪谷）》也是如谜一般，其故事容量之大和结局之神秘，不亚于某些长篇。《哦，姐姐》，一首短如圣谕的歌，它的美仿佛古老的箴言……

《渴望》展现了迪伦与利维惊人的叙事诗才华。诗中所刻画的"受压迫英雄"的形象，可能直观反映了此时迪伦的心境，一种英雄末路、人生失意的悲凉。

《渴望》在录制过程中产生了众多被淘汰的歌曲，这些歌词以附加歌词的形式收录于本书中，共计 7 首。

HURRICANE
(WITH JACQUES LEVY)

Pistol shots ring out in the barroom night
Enter Patty Valentine from the upper hall
She sees the bartender in a pool of blood
Cries out, "My God, they killed them all!"
Here comes the story of the Hurricane
The man the authorities came to blame
For somethin' that he never done
Put in a prison cell, but one time he could-a been
The champion of the world

Three bodies lyin' there does Patty see
And another man named Bello, movin' around mysteriously
"I didn't do it," he says, and he throws up his hands
"I was only robbin' the register, I hope you understand
I saw them leavin'," he says, and he stops
"One of us had better call up the cops"
And so Patty calls the cops
And they arrive on the scene with their red lights flashin'
In the hot New Jersey night

Meanwhile, far away in another part of town

飓风
（与雅克·利维合作）

手枪声在酒吧夜晚响起
帕蒂·瓦伦丁从上层大厅跑下来
看到酒保倒在血泊里
她喊道："我的上帝，他们杀了他们！"
"飓风"的故事由此开始
这个男人被法庭定了罪
为他从未做过的事
投进了班房，本来他可以成为
世界冠军

帕蒂见地上躺着三具尸体
一个叫贝洛的男人，诡异地四处走动
"不是我干的，"他说，举起了双手
"我只是抢收银机，希望你能明白
我看到他们离开了，"说着他停下来
"我们最好有一个人电话报警"
于是帕蒂报了警
警察到了，现场红灯闪烁
在新泽西这个炎热的夜

与此同时，远在城市另一区域

Rubin Carter and a couple of friends are drivin' around
Number one contender for the middleweight crown
Had no idea what kinda shit was about to go down
When a cop pulled him over to the side of the road
Just like the time before and the time before that
In Paterson that's just the way things go
If you're black you might as well not show up on the street
'Less you wanna draw the heat

Alfred Bello had a partner and he had a rap for the cops
Him and Arthur Dexter Bradley were just out prowlin' around
He said, "I saw two men runnin' out, they looked like middleweights
They jumped into a white car with out-of-state plates"
And Miss Patty Valentine just nodded her head
Cop said, "Wait a minute, boys, this one's not dead"
So they took him to the infirmary
And though this man could hardly see
They told him that he could identify the guilty men

Four in the mornin' and they haul Rubin in

鲁宾·卡特[1]和几个朋友开车转悠

中量级拳王的头号争夺者

不知道发生了什么狗屁事

当一名警察把他拉到路边

就像上次和上上次一样

在帕特森,事情就是如此

如果你是黑人,最好不要出现在街上

除非你想引火上身

阿尔弗雷德·贝洛有个同伙,他向警察供述

他和阿瑟·德克斯特·布拉德利当时只是在游荡

他说:"我看到两个男人跑出来,像是中等
  体型

跳进了一辆挂外州牌照的白色小车"

而帕蒂·瓦伦丁小姐只是点了点头

警察说:"等一下,伙计们,这人还没死"

他们把他带到了医务室

虽然这个人几乎失明了

但他们告诉他,他可以指认凶手

凌晨四点,他们把鲁宾拖进来

---

[1] 鲁宾·卡特(1937—2014),美国黑人中量级拳王,因拳风富于侵略性和力量感,获"飓风"绰号。1966 年,他被判谋杀 3 人而入狱,但从未认罪。1985 年,他在不断上诉中被改判无罪而获释。在卡特服刑期间,迪伦阅读了他的自传,并前往探望,与雅克·利维一同创作了这首歌。

Take him to the hospital and they bring him upstairs
The wounded man looks up through his one dyin' eye
Says, "Wha'd you bring him in here for? He ain't the guy!"
Yes, here's the story of the Hurricane
The man the authorities came to blame
For somethin' that he never done
Put in a prison cell, but one time he could-a been
The champion of the world

Four months later, the ghettos are in flame
Rubin's in South America, fightin' for his name
While Arthur Dexter Bradley's still in the robbery game
And the cops are puttin' the screws to him, lookin' for somebody to blame
"Remember that murder that happened in a bar?"
"Remember you said you saw the getaway car?"
"You think you'd like to play ball with the law?"
"Think it might-a been that fighter that you saw runnin' that night?"
"Don't forget that you are white"

Arthur Dexter Bradley said, "I'm really not sure"
Cops said, "A poor boy like you could use a break
We got you for the motel job and we're talkin' to your friend Bello
Now you don't wanta have to go back to jail, be a nice fellow

带他去了医院,又弄上了楼
那伤者抬起头,睁开一只快瞎的眼
说:"你们把他带这儿干吗?他不是那个人!"
是的,"飓风"的故事就从这里开始
这个男人被法庭定了罪
为他从未做过的事
投进了班房,本来他可以成为
世界冠军

四个月后,贫民区一片沸腾
鲁宾在南美洲,为他的名誉而战
而阿瑟·德克斯特·布拉德利仍陷在抢劫案里
警察在对他施压,就为了找人
　顶罪
"还记得酒吧发生的那起凶杀案吧?"
"还记得你说你看到了逃逸的小汽车吧?"
"你觉得你愿意和法律合作吧?"
"想想看那晚你看到的逃犯可能是那个
　拳击手吧?"
"别忘了你是白人"

阿瑟·德克斯特·布拉德利说:"我真的不确定"
警察说:"像你这样可怜的孩子该缓口气了
我们给你找了个汽车旅馆的工作,正在和
　你朋友贝洛谈
既然你不想再坐牢,那就做个好人

You'll be doin' society a favor
That sonofabitch is brave and gettin' braver
We want to put his ass in stir
We want to pin this triple murder on him
He ain't no Gentleman Jim"

Rubin could take a man out with just one punch
But he never did like to talk about it all that much
It's my work, he'd say, and I do it for pay
And when it's over I'd just as soon go on my way
Up to some paradise
Where the trout streams flow and the air is nice
And ride a horse along a trail
But then they took him to the jailhouse
Where they try to turn a man into a mouse

All of Rubin's cards were marked in advance
The trial was a pig-circus, he never had a chance
The judge made Rubin's witnesses drunkards from the slums
To the white folks who watched he was a revolutionary bum
And to the black folks he was just a crazy nigger
No one doubted that he pulled the trigger
And though they could not produce the gun

帮社会一个忙

那个婊子养的很嚣张,越来越嚣张

我们要揍烂他的屁股

我们要把这三重谋杀罪钉他头上

他才不是'绅士吉姆'[1]"

鲁宾可以一拳把对手送出局

但这事他从不乐意多谈

这是我的工作,他会说,这只是干活赚钱

一结束,我就会立即上路

到天堂一样的所在

有鳟鱼溪流,空气清新

沿着小径骑马

但后来他们把他弄进了监狱

把一个人变成了老鼠

鲁宾全部的牌都被事先做了手脚

审判是场"猪马戏",他没有一点机会

法官让鲁宾的证人变成贫民窟的酒鬼

不管是视他为革命流浪汉的白人

还是把他看作发疯的黑鬼的黑人

没有人怀疑他扣动了扳机

虽然他们造不出那把枪

---

[1] 美国重量级拳王詹姆斯·约翰·科贝特被称作"现代拳击之父",因为人正直,被人们称为"绅士吉姆"。

The D.A. said he was the one who did the deed
And the all-white jury agreed

Rubin Carter was falsely tried
The crime was murder "one," guess who testified?
Bello and Bradley and they both baldly lied
And the newspapers, they all went along for the ride
How can the life of such a man
Be in the palm of some fool's hand?
To see him obviously framed
Couldn't help but make me feel ashamed to live in a land
Where justice is a game

Now all the criminals in their coats and their ties
Are free to drink martinis and watch the sun rise
While Rubin sits like Buddha in a ten-foot cell
An innocent man in a living hell
That's the story of the Hurricane
But it won't be over till they clear his name
And give him back the time he's done
Put in a prison cell, but one time he could-a been
The champion of the world

地方检察官说凶案就是他干的
清一色白人陪审团表示同意

鲁宾·卡特被错误审判
罪行是一级谋杀,猜猜谁做证?
贝洛和布拉德利,两人都公然撒谎
还有报纸,全跟着起哄
这样的一个人的生命
怎会落入白痴手中?
看到他明显遭陷害
不禁让我为生活在正义是场游戏的土地上
感到羞耻

现在所有的罪犯都穿正装打领带
自由地喝着马提尼看日出
而鲁宾却像佛陀坐在十英尺的囚室
一个无辜的人,困在活生生的地狱
这就是"飓风"的故事
它不会结束,在他们为他洗清罪名
并把他服刑的时间都还给他之前
若非被投进班房,本来他可以成为
世界冠军

ISIS
(WITH JACQUES LEVY)

I married Isis on the fifth day of May
But I could not hold on to her very long
So I cut off my hair and I rode straight away
For the wild unknown country where I could not go wrong

I came to a high place of darkness and light
The dividing line ran through the center of town
I hitched up my pony to a post on the right
Went in to a laundry to wash my clothes down

A man in the corner approached me for a match
I knew right away he was not ordinary
He said, "Are you lookin' for somethin' easy to catch?"
I said, "I got no money." He said, "That ain't necessary"

We set out that night for the cold in the North
I gave him my blanket, he gave me his word
I said, "Where are we goin'?" He said we'd be back by the fourth
I said, "That's the best news that I've ever heard"

伊西丝

（与雅克·利维合作）

我在五月的第五天和伊西丝结了婚
但我没办法和她长久
所以我剪掉了头发打马直奔荒野
去我不会走错的未知的乡村

我来到那明与暗的高处
分界线从镇子中心穿过
我把小马拴在右边柱子上
去洗衣店洗我的衣服

角落里一个男人凑近向我借火
我立刻就知道他不是一般人
他说："你在找什么容易得手的事？"
我说："我没钱。"他说："钱不必要"

那晚我们出发去寒冷的北方
我把毯子给了他，他给了他的保证
我说："我们去哪儿？"他说第四天
　就回来
我说："这是我听到的最好的消息"

I was thinkin' about turquoise, I was thinkin' about gold
I was thinkin' about diamonds and the world's biggest necklace
As we rode through the canyons, through the devilish cold
I was thinkin' about Isis, how she thought I was so reckless

How she told me that one day we would meet up again
And things would be different the next time we wed
If I only could hang on and just be her friend
I still can't remember all the best things she said

We came to the pyramids all embedded in ice
He said, "There's a body I'm tryin' to find
If I carry it out it'll bring a good price"
'Twas then that I knew what he had on his mind

The wind it was howlin' and the snow was outrageous
We chopped through the night and we chopped through the dawn
When he died I was hopin' that it wasn't contagious
But I made up my mind that I had to go on

I broke into the tomb, but the casket was empty
There was no jewels, no nothin', I felt I'd been had
When I saw that my partner was just bein' friendly
When I took up his offer I must-a been mad

我想到了绿松石，我想到了黄金
我想到了钻石和世界上最大的项链
当我们策马穿过峡谷，穿过恶魔般的寒冷
我想到了伊西丝，她会怎么看待我的鲁莽

她是怎么告诉我有一天我们还会相见
等下次我们结婚一切将会不同
如果我能坚持下去只做她的朋友就好
可我仍然记不起所有她说过的最美好的话

我们到了金字塔下，塔完全嵌在冰里
他说："这里有具我一直在找的木乃伊
把它搬出来就能卖个好价钱"
直到此时我才明白，他肚子里打的主意

风在嚎叫，雪在咆哮
我们凿穿了黑夜，我们凿到了
   拂晓
凿到他死了这霉运可别传染我
但我抱定了决心我必须干下去

我凿进了墓穴，但棺材是空的
没有珠宝，什么也没有，我想象的都没有
我这才看清我的拍档只是面相讨好
而我接受了他的提议我一定是疯了

I picked up his body and I dragged him inside
Threw him down in the hole and I put back the cover
I said a quick prayer and I felt satisfied
Then I rode back to find Isis just to tell her I love her

She was there in the meadow where the creek used to rise
Blinded by sleep and in need of a bed
I came in from the East with the sun in my eyes
I cursed her one time then I rode on ahead

She said, "Where ya been?" I said, "No place special"
She said, "You look different." I said, "Well, not quite"
She said, "You been gone." I said, "That's only natural"
She said, "You gonna stay?" I said, "Yeah, I jes might"

Isis, oh, Isis, you mystical child
What drives me to you is what drives me insane
I still can remember the way that you smiled
On the fifth day of May in the drizzlin' rain

我抱起他的尸体,把他拖进去
扔进棺材把盖子再盖好
我做了简短的祈祷感到满足
然后打马回去找伊西丝只为了告诉她我爱她

她在小溪从前发源的草甸上
被沉沉睡意笼罩,需要一张床
我从东方来太阳在我眼里
那次我诅咒了她然后打马远去

她说:"你去哪儿?"我说:"不值一提"
她说:"你不一样了。"我说:"嗯,不完全是"
她说:"你走了。"我说:"这很自然"
她说:"你要留下来?"我说:"是的,可能吧"

伊西丝,啊,伊西丝,你这神秘的孩子
是什么让我走向你,也是什么教我发疯
我依然记得你微笑的样子
在五月第五天的蒙蒙细雨里

MOZAMBIQUE
(WITH JACQUES LEVY)

I like to spend some time in Mozambique
The sunny sky is aqua blue
And all the couples dancing cheek to cheek
It's very nice to stay a week or two

There's lot of pretty girls in Mozambique
And plenty time for good romance
And everybody likes to stop and speak
To give the special one you seek a chance
Or maybe say hello with just a glance

Lying next to her by the ocean
Reaching out and touching her hand
Whispering your secret emotion
Magic in a magical land

And when it's time for leaving Mozambique
To say goodbye to sand and sea
You turn around to take a final peek
And you see why it's so unique to be
Among the lovely people living free
Upon the beach of sunny Mozambique

莫桑比克
（与雅克·利维合作）

我喜欢在莫桑比克花时间
晴朗的天水一样湛蓝
双双对对的人脸贴脸跳舞
待上一两个星期真是太好了

莫桑比克美女如云
大把的时光足够浪漫
人人都爱停下来聊两句
这给你找寻妙人儿一个机会
又或者只是说声好对下眼

躺在她身边，大海在眼前
伸伸手就摸到她的手
低低轻诉你的秘密情感
魔幻大地魔力弥漫

又到了离开莫桑比克的时候
要跟沙滩和海说再见了
转过身看那最后一眼
你明白了它为何妙绝人寰
一大片都是自由可爱的人
一大片都是阳光灿烂的莫桑比克海岸

ONE MORE CUP OF COFFEE
(VALLEY BELOW)

Your breath is sweet
Your eyes are like two jewels in the sky
Your back is straight, your hair is smooth
On the pillow where you lie
But I don't sense affection
No gratitude or love
Your loyalty is not to me
But to the stars above

One more cup of coffee for the road
One more cup of coffee 'fore I go
To the valley below

Your daddy he's an outlaw
And a wanderer by trade
He'll teach you how to pick and choose
And how to throw the blade
He oversees his kingdom
So no stranger does intrude

再喝一杯咖啡
（下面的溪谷）[1]

你气息甜美
眼睛像苍穹中的两颗宝石
你脊背笔直，头发在枕间
柔滑如丝
可是我感觉不到情义
不见感激，也未见爱情
你属意的不是我
你属意的是上面的星辰

再喝一杯咖啡就上路
再喝一杯咖啡我就走入
这下面的溪谷

你爹是一个亡命徒
为了生意他四处漂泊
他将教会你挑选
教你如何抛掷飞刀
他掌管他的王国
陌生人概莫能入

---

[1] 本篇由杨盈盈校译。

His voice it trembles as he calls out
For another plate of food

One more cup of coffee for the road
One more cup of coffee 'fore I go
To the valley below

Your sister sees the future
Like your mama and yourself
You've never learned to read or write
There's no books upon your shelf
And your pleasure knows no limits
Your voice is like a meadowlark
But your heart is like an ocean
Mysterious and dark

One more cup of coffee for the road
One more cup of coffee 'fore I go
To the valley below

他声音颤抖地吆喝
唤来下一盘食物

再喝一杯咖啡就上路
再喝一杯咖啡我就走入
这下面的溪谷

你妹妹能看到未来
跟你妈和你一样
你没读过书也不会写字
书架上空空荡荡
而你的欢乐无穷无尽
你的嗓音就像百灵
但是你的心像片海
神秘又黑暗

再喝一杯咖啡就上路
再喝一杯咖啡我就走入
这下面的溪谷

OH, SISTER
(WITH JACQUES LEVY)

Oh, sister, when I come to lie in your arms
You should not treat me like a stranger
Our Father would not like the way that you act
And you must realize the danger

Oh, sister, am I not a brother to you
And one deserving of affection?
And is our purpose not the same on this earth
To love and follow His direction?

We grew up together
From the cradle to the grave
We died and were reborn
And then mysteriously saved

Oh, sister, when I come to knock on your door
Don't turn away, you'll create sorrow
Time is an ocean but it ends at the shore
You may not see me tomorrow

哦,姐姐
(与雅克·利维合作)

哦,姐姐,当我投入你的怀抱
你不该把我当外人
我们的父不喜欢你这样
你必须意识到危险

哦,姐姐,莫非我不是你的兄弟
一个值得爱的人?
莫非我们在这世上的目的不一样
不是要去爱并追随他的方向?

我们一起长大
从摇篮到坟墓
我们死过了又重生
然后神秘地得救

哦,姐姐,当我走过来敲你的门
别转身,那会制造悔恨
时光是大海,可它在岸边终结
明天你可能见不到我

JOEY
(WITH JACQUES LEVY)

Born in Red Hook, Brooklyn, in the year of who knows when
Opened up his eyes to the tune of an accordion
Always on the outside of whatever side there was
When they asked him why it had to be that way, "Well,"
   he answered,
"just because"

Larry was the oldest, Joey was next to last
They called Joe "Crazy," the baby they called "Kid Blast"
Some say they lived off gambling and runnin' numbers too
It always seemed they got caught between the mob and the
   men in blue

Joey, Joey
King of the streets, child of clay
Joey, Joey

乔伊 [1]
（与雅克·利维合作）

生于布鲁克林的雷德胡克，天晓得哪一年
随着手风琴的声音他睁开眼
永远在局外，不在任一方
他们问他为什么非这样。"嗯，"
   他回答，
"不为什么"

拉里是老大，乔伊排行次末
他们叫他"疯狂乔"，叫老幺"爆炸小子"
有人说他们干的是赌博和跑码 [2] 的活儿
似乎总是夹在黑道和警察
   之间

乔伊，乔伊
街头之王，泥土之子
乔伊，乔伊

---

[1] 乔伊·加洛（1929—1972），纽约黑手党普罗法齐家族的帮派成员，1972 年死于谋杀。
[2] 跑码，指博彩生意中，从码民那里收取赌注、投注号码及派发奖金的活儿。

What made them want to come and blow you away?

There was talk they killed their rivals, but the truth was far from that
No one ever knew for sure where they were really at
When they tried to strangle Larry, Joey almost hit the roof
He went out that night to seek revenge, thinkin' he was bulletproof

The war broke out at the break of dawn, it emptied out the streets
Joey and his brothers suffered terrible defeats
Till they ventured out behind the lines and took five prisoners
They stashed them away in a basement, called them amateurs

The hostages were tremblin' when they heard a man exclaim
"Let's blow this place to kingdom come, let Con Edison take the blame"
But Joey stepped up, he raised his hand, said, "We're not those kind of men
It's peace and quiet that we need to go back to work again"

Joey, Joey
King of the streets, child of clay
Joey, Joey
What made them want to come and blow you away?

是什么让他们想除掉你?

传言说他们干掉了自己的对手,但这
    远非事实
没人确切知道当时他们真正在哪儿
当他们意图勒死拉里,乔伊差点儿撞翻屋顶
当晚他出去报仇,自以为
    刀枪不入

激战爆发于破晓,几条街
    空无一人
乔伊和弟兄们惨败
直到他们冒险冲到后方抓了五个俘虏
把俘虏藏进地下室,称他们"生瓜蛋子"

五名人质浑身发抖,当他们听到有个人喊
"把这地方炸上天,让联合爱迪生
    去背锅"
但是乔伊走上前,抬起手说:"我们不是
    那路人
我们要的是和平与宁静,重新回去工作"

乔伊,乔伊
街头之王,泥土之子
乔伊,乔伊
是什么让他们想除掉你?

The police department hounded him, they called him Mr. Smith
They got him on conspiracy, they were never sure who with
"What time is it?" said the judge to Joey when they met
"Five to ten," said Joey. The judge says, "That's exactly what you get"

He did ten years in Attica, reading Nietzsche and Wilhelm Reich
They threw him in the hole one time for tryin' to stop a strike
His closest friends were black men 'cause they seemed to understand
What it's like to be in society with a shackle on your hand

When they let him out in '71 he'd lost a little weight
But he dressed like Jimmy Cagney and I swear he did look great
He tried to find the way back into the life he left behind
To the boss he said, "I have returned and now I want what's mine"

Joey, Joey

警方追捕他,称他史密斯先生
他们以同谋罪抓了他,却从不确定是跟谁
"现在几点?"见面时法官问乔伊
"差五分十点[1]。"乔伊说。法官说:"这正是你
　之所得"

他在阿提卡服刑十年,读尼采和
　威廉·赖希[2]
有次他们把他关进小房,以阻止一场罢工
他最亲密的朋友是黑人,因为黑人们
　似乎懂得
手戴枷锁在社会上是什么感觉

七一年放他出去时,他瘦了些许
但他穿得像吉米·卡格尼[3],我发誓他看上去确实棒
他要想办法重回他阔别已久的生活
他对老板说:"我回来了,现在我要回我的
　东西"

乔伊,乔伊

---

[1] 差五分十点,双关语,与"五到十年"表述相同。
[2] 威廉·赖希(1897—1957),美籍奥地利心理学家、社会学家,被视为美国20世纪四五十年代性解放运动的精神领袖之一。
[3] 吉米·卡格尼,美国演员。

King of the streets, child of clay
Joey, Joey
Why did they have to come and blow you away?

It was true that in his later years he would not carry a gun
"I'm around too many children," he'd say, "they should never know of one"
Yet he walked right into the clubhouse of his lifelong deadly foe
Emptied out the register, said, "Tell 'em it was Crazy Joe"

One day they blew him down in a clam bar in New York
He could see it comin' through the door as he lifted up his fork
He pushed the table over to protect his family
Then he staggered out into the streets of Little Italy

Joey, Joey
King of the streets, child of clay
Joey, Joey
What made them want to come and blow you away?

Sister Jacqueline and Carmela and mother Mary all did weep
I heard his best friend Frankie say, "He ain't dead, he's just asleep"
Then I saw the old man's limousine head back towards the grave
I guess he had to say one last goodbye to the son that he could

街头之王,泥土之子
乔伊,乔伊
是什么让他们想除掉你?

这是真的,在人生最后的岁月他不愿带枪
"我身边有太多孩子,"他说,"他们该永远
　不知道这个"
然而他却径直走进他终生死敌的会所
清空了收银机,说:"告诉他们是疯狂乔干的"

有一天,他们在纽约一家蛤蜊餐馆除掉了他
他拿起叉子时看到灾祸进了门
他掀翻桌子以保护家人
然后跌跌撞撞冲进小意大利的街道

乔伊,乔伊
街头之王,泥土之子
乔伊,乔伊
是什么让他们想除掉你?

姐姐杰奎琳、卡梅拉和母亲玛丽都哭了
我听到他最好的朋友弗兰基说:"他没死,他只是
　睡着了"
然后我看到老人的豪华车掉转头开向
　墓地
我猜他要去说最后一次再见,和他没能救

163

   not save

The sun turned cold over President Street and the town of
   Brooklyn mourned
They said a mass in the old church near the house where he
   was born
And someday if God's in heaven overlookin' His preserve
I know the men that shot him down will get what they deserve

Joey, Joey
King of the streets, child of clay
Joey, Joey
What made them want to come and blow you away?

回来的儿子

太阳在总统街变冷,布鲁克林悲雾
　沉沉
他们说弥撒在老教堂,就在他出生的
　房子附近
如果有一天上帝在天堂俯瞰他保佑的世界
我知道枪杀他的人会得到应有的报应

乔伊,乔伊
街头之王,泥土之子
乔伊,乔伊
是什么让他们想除掉你?

ROMANCE IN DURANGO
(WITH JACQUES LEVY)

Hot chili peppers in the blistering sun
Dust on my face and my cape
Me and Magdalena on the run
I think this time we shall escape

Sold my guitar to the baker's son
For a few crumbs and a place to hide
But I can get another one
And I'll play for Magdalena as we ride

No llores, mi querida
Dios nos vigila
Soon the horse will take us to Durango
Agarrame, mi vida
Soon the desert will be gone
Soon you will be dancing the fandango

杜兰戈罗曼史

（与雅克·利维合作）

红辣椒在炎炎烈日中
尘土在我的脸和斗篷上
我和玛格达莱娜在跑
我想这回我们一定能逃掉

我把吉他卖给了面包师的儿子
换了些面包渣和一个藏身之所
但我还能再弄一把
我会在骑马时弹给玛格达莱娜

亲爱的，别哭
神在看顾我们
很快马儿会把我们带到杜兰戈 [1]
抱紧我，我的生命
很快沙漠将走过
很快你就会跳起方丹戈 [2]

---

[1] 杜兰戈，墨西哥中北部城市，迪伦曾在这里参与拍摄电影《帕特·加勒特和比利小子》。
[2] 方丹戈，一种西班牙舞。

Past the Aztec ruins and the ghosts of our people
Hoofbeats like castanets on stone
At night I dream of bells in the village steeple
Then I see the bloody face of Ramon

Was it me that shot him down in the cantina
Was it my hand that held the gun?
Come, let us fly, my Magdalena
The dogs are barking and what's done is done

No llores, mi querida
Dios nos vigila
Soon the horse will take us to Durango
Agarrame, mi vida
Soon the desert will be gone
Soon you will be dancing the fandango

At the corrida we'll sit in the shade
And watch the young torero stand alone
We'll drink tequila where our grandfathers stayed
When they rode with Villa into Torreón

Then the padre will recite the prayers of old

走过阿兹特克的废墟和吾民的魂
马蹄声声如石上的响板
夜里我梦到村庄尖塔的钟声
然后看到拉蒙血淋淋的脸

是我把他在饭馆撂倒的吗?
握枪的是我的手吗?
来吧,让我们飞,我的玛格达莱娜
狗在叫,干了就干了

亲爱的,别哭
神在看顾我们
很快马儿会把我们带到杜兰戈
抱紧我,我的生命
很快沙漠将走过
很快你就会跳起方丹戈

在斗牛场我们会坐在浓荫里
注视年轻的斗牛士孤身独立
我们会喝龙舌兰,我们的祖父也曾在那里
当年他们和比利亚[1]骑马进入托雷翁

然后神父会高诵古老的祷文

---

[1] 比利亚,即潘乔·比利亚,墨西哥革命时期领袖,1911 年 5 月 15 日率军攻入托雷翁城。

In the little church this side of town
I will wear new boots and an earring of gold
You'll shine with diamonds in your wedding gown

The way is long but the end is near
Already the fiesta has begun
The face of God will appear
With His serpent eyes of obsidian

No llores, mi querida
Dio nos vigila
Soon the horse will take us to Durango
Agarrame, mi vida
Soon the desert will be gone
Soon you will be dancing the fandango

Was that the thunder that I heard?
My head is vibrating, I feel a sharp pain
Come sit by me, don't say a word
Oh, can it be that I am slain?

Quick, Magdalena, take my gun
Look up in the hills, that flash of light

就在小镇这边的小教堂中
我会穿新靴戴上一只金耳环
你会披上婚纱钻石闪闪

路很长但终点很近
盛会已经开始
上帝的脸将显现
投射过来他黑曜石的蛇眼

亲爱的,别哭
神在看顾我们[1]
很快马儿会把我们带到杜兰戈
抱紧我,我的生命
很快沙漠将走过
很快你就会跳起方丹戈

我听到的是雷霆吗?
我的头在抖,我感到一阵剧痛
来坐我身边,什么都不说
啊,难道是我被杀了?

快,玛格达莱娜,拿起我的枪
抬头看群山上,那一闪而过的光

---

[1] "亲爱的别哭/神在看顾我们""抱紧我,我的生命"这两句,原文为西班牙语。

Aim well my little one

We may not make it through the night

No llores, mi querida

Dios nos vigila

Soon the horse will take us to Durango

Agarrame, mi vida

Soon the desert will be gone

Soon you will be dancing the fandango

瞄准好我的小甜甜
我们可能熬不过今晚

亲爱的，别哭
神在看顾我们
很快马儿会把我们带到杜兰戈
抱紧我，我的生命
很快沙漠将走过
很快你就会跳起方丹戈

BLACK DIAMOND BAY
(WITH JACQUES LEVY)

Up on the white veranda

She wears a necktie and a Panama hat

Her passport shows a face

From another time and place

She looks nothin' like that

And all the remnants of her recent past

Are scattered in the wild wind

She walks across the marble floor

Where a voice from the gambling room is callin' her to come
on in

She smiles, walks the other way

As the last ship sails and the moon fades away

From Black Diamond Bay

As the mornin' light breaks open, the Greek comes down

And he asks for a rope and a pen that will write

"Pardon, monsieur," the desk clerk says

Carefully removes his fez

"Am I hearin' you right?"

黑钻石湾

(与雅克·利维合作)

白色游廊上
她系着领带,戴顶巴拿马帽
护照显示另一张脸
来自另一时空
看起来和她一点儿不像
而她近一段日子的所有余烬
都散落在狂风中
她走过大理石地面
赌场中传来声音叫她
 进去
她笑了笑,转身走了
此时最后一艘船启航,月亮隐去
从黑钻石湾

晨光刺破苍穹,希腊人走下楼
要一根绳子和一支笔
"不好意思,先生,"[1] 前台小伙说
小心地摘下毡帽
"我没听错吧?"

---

[1] "不好意思,先生,"本句部分原文为法语。

And as the yellow fog is liftin'
The Greek is quickly headin' for the second floor
She passes him on the spiral staircase
Thinkin' he's the Soviet Ambassador
She starts to speak, but he walks away
As the storm clouds rise and the palm branches sway
On Black Diamond Bay

A soldier sits beneath the fan
Doin' business with a tiny man who sells him a ring
Lightning strikes, the lights blow out
The desk clerk wakes and begins to shout
"Can you see anything?"
Then the Greek appears on the second floor
In his bare feet with a rope around his neck
While a loser in the gambling room lights up a candle
Says, "Open up another deck"
But the dealer says, "Attendez-vous, s'il vous plaît"
As the rain beats down and the cranes fly away
From Black Diamond Bay

The desk clerk heard the woman laugh
As he looked around the aftermath and the soldier got tough
He tried to grab the woman's hand

随着黄色雾气消散
希腊人快速走上二楼
她在旋梯上与他交错
以为他是那个苏联大使
她正开口,但他走开了
此时暴风云起,棕榈树枝摇曳
在黑钻石湾

一名士兵坐在风扇下
在和卖他戒指的小个子谈生意
雷电闪过,电灯骤熄
前台小伙惊醒,叫嚷起来
"你们能看见吗?"
然后希腊人出现在二楼
光着脚,脖子上套着绳索
赌场里输家点亮蜡烛
说:"再开一副牌吧"
但庄家说:"请再等等"[1]
此时大雨倾盆,黄鹤飞去
从黑钻石湾

前台小伙听到女人笑起来
他扫视四周,士兵正变得强硬
要去抓女人的手

---

[1] "请再等等",本句原文为法语。

Said, "Here's a ring, it cost a grand"

She said, "That ain't enough"

Then she ran upstairs to pack her bags

While a horse-drawn taxi waited at the curb

She passed the door that the Greek had locked

Where a handwritten sign read, "Do Not Disturb"

She knocked upon it anyway

As the sun went down and the music did play

On Black Diamond Bay

"I've got to talk to someone quick!"

But the Greek said, "Go away," and he kicked the chair to the floor

He hung there from the chandelier

She cried, "Help, there's danger near

Please open up the door!"

Then the volcano erupted

And the lava flowed down from the mountain high above

The soldier and the tiny man were crouched in the corner

Thinking of forbidden love

But the desk clerk said, "It happens every day"

As the stars fell down and the fields burned away

On Black Diamond Bay

As the island slowly sank

The loser finally broke the bank in the gambling room

说:"这有枚戒指,花了一大笔"
她说:"还不够"
说完跑上楼收拾行李
一辆出租马车等在路边
她从希腊人紧锁的门前经过
门上有手写的字条"请勿打扰"
她还是敲了门
此时太阳落下,音乐响起
在黑钻石湾

"我得马上找人谈谈"
但希腊人说"走开",然后
　　踢翻了椅子
把自己吊在吊灯上
她喊道:"救命,来人哪
请打开门!"
然后火山爆发了
熔岩从高高的山上流下
士兵和小个子蹲在角落
想着那禁忌之爱
但前台小伙说:"天天都是这样"
此时群星坠落,田野烧成白地
在黑钻石湾

小岛缓缓下沉
赌场里,输家终于洗清了盘面

The dealer said, "It's too late now

You can take your money, but I don't know how

You'll spend it in the tomb"

The tiny man bit the soldier's ear

As the floor caved in and the boiler in the basement blew

While she's out on the balcony, where a stranger tells her

"My darling, je vous aime beaucoup"

She sheds a tear and then begins to pray

As the fire burns on and the smoke drifts away

From Black Diamond Bay

I was sittin' home alone one night in L.A.

Watchin' old Cronkite on the seven o'clock news

It seems there was an earthquake that

Left nothin' but a Panama hat

And a pair of old Greek shoes

Didn't seem like much was happenin'

So I turned it off and went to grab another beer

Seems like every time you turn around

There's another hard-luck story that you're gonna hear

And there's really nothin' anyone can say

And I never did plan to go anyway

To Black Diamond Bay

庄家说:"已经太迟
你可以拿走钱,可我不知道
在坟墓里你怎么花掉"
小个子咬了士兵的耳朵
此时地板坍塌,地下室的锅炉爆炸
而她跑到阳台外,一个陌生人对她说
"亲爱的,我非常爱你"
她掉下一滴泪,然后开始祈祷
此时大火熊熊,烟雾弥漫
从黑钻石湾

洛杉矶一个晚上,我一个人坐在家里
看老克朗凯特[1]的七点新闻
好像说发生了地震
现场什么都不剩,除了一顶巴拿马帽
和一双旧希腊鞋
貌似不是多大的事
所以我关掉电视,又取了一瓶啤酒
好像每一次你转身
都会有又一个要听的倒霉事
也真的没人能说什么
而且不管如何,我都没计划过
要去黑钻石湾

---

[1] 克朗凯特,美国著名记者,1962 至 1981 年任哥伦比亚广播公司《晚间新闻》主播,被誉为"美国最受信任的人"。

SARA

I laid on a dune, I looked at the sky
When the children were babies and played on the beach
You came up behind me, I saw you go by
You were always so close and still within reach

Sara, Sara
Whatever made you want to change your mind?
Sara, Sara
So easy to look at, so hard to define

I can still see them playin' with their pails in the sand
They run to the water their buckets to fill
I can still see the shells fallin' out of their hands
As they follow each other back up the hill

Sara, Sara
Sweet virgin angel, sweet love of my life
Sara, Sara
Radiant jewel, mystical wife

Sleepin' in the woods by a fire in the night
Drinkin' white rum in a Portugal bar

萨拉

我躺在沙丘上,望着天
那时孩子们还小,在沙滩玩
你来到了我身后,我看着你走过
你总是那么近,仍然触手可及

萨拉,萨拉
是什么让你改变心意?
萨拉,萨拉
眼望你如此容易,描画却是难题

我仍然能看见孩子们在沙滩玩桶
他们跑向大海让小桶灌满
我仍然能看见贝壳从他们手中滑落
当他们一个跟一个回到山间

萨拉,萨拉
甜蜜的圣洁天使,甜蜜的我一生之爱
萨拉,萨拉
璀璨的宝石,神秘的妻

夜晚在林中篝火边入眠
在葡萄牙酒吧喝白朗姆

Them playin' leapfrog and hearin' about Snow White
You in the marketplace in Savanna-la-Mar

Sara, Sara
It's all so clear, I could never forget
Sara, Sara
Lovin' you is the one thing I'll never regret

I can still hear the sounds of those Methodist bells
I'd taken the cure and had just gotten through
Stayin' up for days in the Chelsea Hotel
Writin' "Sad-Eyed Lady of the Lowlands" for you

Sara, Sara
Wherever we travel we're never apart
Sara, oh Sara
Beautiful lady, so dear to my heart

How did I meet you? I don't know
A messenger sent me in a tropical storm
You were there in the winter, moonlight on the snow
And on Lily Pond Lane when the weather was warm

Sara, oh Sara

孩子们玩跳蛙听《白雪公主》
你在滨海稀树草原的集市里

萨拉,萨拉
一切历历在目,我永远不会忘记
萨拉,萨拉
爱你,是我永不会后悔的事

我仍然能听见卫理公会的钟声
我接受了疗愈,才把难关渡过去
在切尔西酒店彻夜不眠
为你谱写《低地的愁容女士》

萨拉,萨拉
无论走到哪儿,我们永不分离
萨拉,啊萨拉
我心中的至爱,美丽的女士

我是怎么遇上你的?我不知道
一个信使把我送进了热带风暴
你到那里时是冬天,月光映在雪上
而在荷塘巷 [1] 时,天气温暖

萨拉,啊萨拉

---

[1] 荷塘巷,纽约州东汉普顿附近的住宅区。

Scorpio Sphinx in a calico dress
Sara, Sara
You must forgive me my unworthiness

Now the beach is deserted except for some kelp
And a piece of an old ship that lies on the shore
You always responded when I needed your help
You gimme a map and a key to your door

Sara, oh Sara
Glamorous nymph with an arrow and bow
Sara, oh Sara
Don't ever leave me, don't ever go

穿印花长裙的斯芬克斯天蝎
萨拉，萨拉
你必须原谅我的不配

如今那沙滩只剩下一些海草
还有在岸边一艘旧船的残迹
我需要你帮助时你总会回应
给我一张地图和一把你房门的钥匙

萨拉，啊萨拉
手持弓箭的妩媚的森林女神
萨拉，啊萨拉
别离开我，永远留在这里

ABANDONED LOVE

I can hear the turning of the key
I've been deceived by the clown inside of me
I thought that he was righteous but he's vain
Oh, something's a-telling me I wear the ball and chain

My patron saint is a-fighting with a ghost
He's always off somewhere when I need him most
The Spanish moon is rising on the hill
But my heart is a-tellin' me I love ya still

I come back to the town from the flaming moon
I see you in the streets, I begin to swoon
I love to see you dress before the mirror
Won't you let me in your room one time 'fore I finally
    disappear?

Everybody's wearing a disguise
To hide what they've got left behind their eyes
But me, I can't cover what I am
Wherever the children go I'll follow them

I march in the parade of liberty

被遗弃的爱

我能听见钥匙转动
我被我内心的小丑欺骗
我以为他正直,可是他虚荣
啊,有些事告诉我,我戴着锁链

我的守护神跟一个幽灵作战
他总在最需要时弃我而去
西班牙的月在山巅升起
但我的心告诉我,我依然爱你

我从燃烧的月亮回到城市
我在街上看到你,我开始晕厥
我喜欢看你镜前梳妆
在我最终消失前,你就不能让我进你
　房间一次?

人人都戴上假面
以遮掩他们丢在眼睛后的东西
但是我,我无法遮掩我的真容
我会跟着孩子们,不管他们去哪里

我加入了自由的游行

But as long as I love you I'm not free

How long must I suffer such abuse

Won't you let me see you smile one time before I turn you loose?

I've given up the game, I've got to leave

The pot of gold is only make-believe

The treasure can't be found by men who search

Whose gods are dead and whose queens are in the church

We sat in an empty theater and we kissed

I asked ya please to cross me off-a your list

My head tells me it's time to make a change

But my heart is telling me I love ya but you're strange

One more time at midnight, near the wall

Take off your heavy makeup and your shawl

Won't you descend from the throne, from where you sit?

Let me feel your love one more time before I abandon it

但只要我爱你,我就不自由
这样的虐待我还要忍多久
在我放手前,你就不能让我看你
　　笑一次?

我已放弃这游戏,我必须离开
黄金罐[1] 只是种虚构
寻宝人无法找到宝物
他们的众神已死,他们的女王在教堂里

我们坐在空荡荡的剧院亲吻
我请求你把我从你名单上划去
我的头脑告诉我是时候要做出改变了
可我的心告诉我我爱你虽然你是陌生的

又一次在午夜,在大墙边
你卸下你的浓妆和你的披肩
你就不能从宝座上、从你的坐处下来吗?
在我放弃之前再感受一次你的爱恋

---

[1] 黄金罐,爱尔兰民间传说,小矮妖在彩虹尽头藏着装满黄金和财宝的坛罐。

CATFISH
(WITH JACQUES LEVY)

Lazy stadium night
Catfish on the mound
"Strike three," the umpire said
Batter have to go back and sit down

Catfish, million-dollar-man
Nobody can throw the ball like Catfish can

Used to work on Mr. Finley's farm
But the old man wouldn't pay
So he packed his glove and took his arm
An' one day he just ran away

Catfish, million-dollar-man
Nobody can throw the ball like Catfish can

Come up where the Yankees are
Dress up in a pinstripe suit
Smoke a custom-made cigar

鲇鱼 [1]
（与雅克·利维合作）

慵懒的体育场之夜
鲇鱼在投球区
"三振出局。"裁判说
击球手只得退场坐下

鲇鱼，百万身价
没人能像鲇鱼那样投球

在芬利先生的农场工作
但是老头不付薪水
所以他收拾好手套带上装备
在某天逃离

鲇鱼，百万身价
没人能像鲇鱼那样投球

进了洋基队俱乐部
穿上细条纹正装
抽定制雪茄

---

[1] "鲇鱼"是棒球明星詹姆斯·亨特（1949—1999）的绰号。

Wear an alligator boot

Catfish, million-dollar-man
Nobody can throw the ball like Catfish can

Carolina born and bred
Love to hunt the little quail
Got a hundred-acre spread
Got some huntin' dogs for sale

Catfish, million-dollar-man
Nobody can throw the ball like Catfish can

Reggie Jackson at the plate
Seein' nothin' but the curve
Swing too early or too late
Got to eat what Catfish serve

Catfish, million-dollar-man
Nobody can throw the ball like Catfish can

Even Billy Martin grins
When the Fish is in the game
Every season twenty wins
Gonna make the Hall of Fame

脚蹬鳄鱼皮靴

鲇鱼,百万身价
没人能像鲇鱼那样投球

在卡罗来纳土生土长
喜欢打小鹌鹑
有一百英亩土地
有一些猎犬待售

鲇鱼,百万身价
没人能像鲇鱼那样投球

雷吉·杰克逊在本垒
只看见了曲线
挥棒不是早就是晚
只好吃鲇鱼的球

鲇鱼,百万身价
没人能像鲇鱼那样投球

连比利·马丁都笑了
只要鲇鱼在场上
每赛季赢二十场
就要进入名人堂

Catfish, million-dollar-man
Nobody can throw the ball like Catfish can

鲇鱼，百万身价
没人能像鲇鱼那样投球

GOLDEN LOOM

Smoky autumn night, stars up in the sky
I see the sailin' boats across the bay go by
Eucalyptus trees hang above the street
And then I turn my head, for you're approachin' me
Moonlight on the water, fisherman's daughter, floatin' in to my room
With a golden loom

First we wash our feet near the immortal shrine
And then our shadows meet and then we drink the wine
I see the hungry clouds up above your face
And then the tears roll down, what a bitter taste
And then you drift away on a summer's day where the wildflowers bloom
With your golden loom

I walk across the bridge in the dismal light
Where all the cars are stripped between the gates of night

金纺车 [1]

烟迷秋夜,星辰在天
我看见海湾对面有帆船驶过
桉树空悬于街道上端
然后我转头,因为你在向我靠近
月光映在水上,渔夫的女儿,飘进
　我房里
带来了一架金纺车

我们先是在永世的神庙旁濯足
然后我们的影子相遇,然后我们共饮
我看见你脸上升起饥渴的云
而后泪珠滚滚,多么苦涩
而后你飘走了,在一个野花绽放的
　夏日
带走了你的金纺车

我在郁郁灯光中走过大桥
夜的两道大门间,所有汽车被抽离

---

[1] 北欧神话中,命运三女神主要做两件事:照看生命之树和用金纺车编织命运之网;《格林童话》中也出现了金纺车。金纺车是与爱情、命运高度相关的意象。

I see the trembling lion with the lotus flower tail

And then I kiss your lips as I lift your veil

But you're gone and then all I seem to recall is the smell of perfume

And your golden loom

我看见战栗的狮子,有莲花的尾
然后我撩起面纱,吻你的唇
可是你走了此后我能记起的似乎只有
　香水味
还有你的金纺车

RITA MAY
(WITH JACQUES LEVY)

Rita May, Rita May
You got your body in the way
You're so damn nonchalant
But it's your mind that I want
You got me huffin' and a-puffin'
Next to you I feel like nothin'
Rita May

Rita May, Rita May
How'd you ever get that way?
When do you ever see the light?
Don't you ever feel a fright?
You got me burnin' and I'm turnin'
But I know I must be learnin'
Rita May

All my friends have told me
If I hang around with you

丽塔·梅[1]
（与雅克·利维合作）

丽塔·梅，丽塔·梅
你用身体挡道
真他妈的冷漠之极
可你的思想正是我要的
你让我气喘吁吁
在你旁边我啥也不是
丽塔·梅

丽塔·梅，丽塔·梅
你怎么会变成了这样？
你什么时候见过光？
你从不害怕吗？
你让我燃烧，我正在转向
而我知道我必须学习
丽塔·梅

所有朋友都告诫我
若我和你相处

---

[1] 丽塔·梅，常被认为指丽塔·梅·布朗（1944—），美国作家，和平主义者和女性主义者。

That I'll go blind
But I know that when you hold me
That there really must be somethin'
On your mind

Rita May, Rita May
Laying in a stack of hay
Do you remember where you been?
What's that crazy place you're in?
I'm gonna have to go to college
'Cause you are the book of knowledge
Rita May

我就会变盲目
但我知道你抱我时
一定真有什么
在你头脑里

丽塔·梅,丽塔·梅
躺在一堆干草中
你是否记得去过哪里?
你现在又在怎样的疯狂之地?
我要去上大学
因为你是知识之书
丽塔·梅

SEVEN DAYS

Seven days, seven more days she'll be comin'
I'll be waiting at the station for her to arrive
Seven more days, all I gotta do is survive

She been gone ever since I been a child
Ever since I seen her smile, I ain't forgotten her eyes
She had a face that could outshine the sun in the skies

I been good, I been good while I been waitin'
Maybe guilty of hesitatin', I just been holdin' on
Seven more days, all that'll be gone

There's kissing in the valley
Thieving in the alley
Fighting every inch of the way
Trying to be tender
With somebody I remember
In a night that's always brighter'n the day

Seven days, seven more days that are connected
Just like I expected, she'll be comin' on forth
My beautiful comrade from the north

七天

七天,再有七天她就来了
我会去车站迎她
还有七天,我要做的就是活下去

她走时我还是个孩子
自从见她笑,她的眼睛再也忘不掉
她有一张比天上的太阳更夺目的脸庞

我还好,等待的时光还好
也许是犹豫的愧疚,让我一直在坚持
再过七天,一切都会过去

在山谷亲吻
在小巷偷窃
路上争夺每一寸
努力变得温柔
对我记忆中的人
在一个总是比白天更亮的夜晚

七天,又一个七天相连
就像我预料的,她还在继续前进
我的自北方而来的美丽伙伴

There's kissing in the valley

Thieving in the alley

Fighting every inch of the way

Trying to be tender

With somebody I remember

In a night that's always brighter'n the day

在山谷亲吻
在小巷偷窃
路上争夺每一寸
努力变得温柔
对我记忆中的人
在一个总是比白天更亮的夜晚

SIGN LANGUAGE

You speak to me
In sign language
As I'm eating a sandwich
In a small café
At a quarter to three
But I can't respond
To your sign language
You're taking advantage
Bringing me down
Can't you make any sound?

'Twas there by the bakery
Surrounded by fakery
Tell her my story
Still I'm still there
Does she know I still care?

Link Wray was playin'

手语

你跟我说话
用手语
我在吃三明治
在小咖啡馆
差一刻三点
可我无法回应
你的手语
你利用了这一点
让我沮丧
你就不能发出点声音吗?

就在面包店旁
四周都是假货
跟她讲我的故事
我仍在那里
她知不知道我还在乎?

林克·雷 [1] 在演奏

---

[1] 林克·雷,常用电吉他以很大的音量演奏。点唱机放出来的音乐很吵,所以听不见对方说的话,以致误会。这音响也代表着摇滚乐,所以后面"他(林克·雷)对我没有好处"一语双关,指涉迪伦从民谣转向电声摇滚。

On a jukebox I was payin'
For the words I was sayin'
So misunderstood
He didn't do me no good

You speak to me
In sign language
As I'm eating a sandwich
In a small café
At a quarter to three
But I can't respond
To your sign language
You're taking advantage
Bringing me down
Can't you make any sound?

在我投币的点唱机
所以我说的话
全被误解了
他对我没有好处

你跟我说话
用手语
我在吃三明治
在小咖啡馆
差一刻三点
可我无法回应
你的手语
你利用了这一点
让我沮丧
你就不能发出点声音吗?

MONEY BLUES
(WITH JACQUES LEVY)

Sittin' here thinkin'
Where does the money go
Sittin' here thinkin'
Where does the money go
Well, I give it to my woman
She ain't got it no more

Went out last night
Bought two eggs and a slice of ham
Went out last night
Bought two eggs and a slice of ham
Bill came to three dollars and ten cents
And I didn't even get no jam

Man came around
Askin' for the rent
Man came around
Askin' for the rent
Well, I looked into the drawer
But the money's all been spent

金钱蓝调
（与雅克·利维合作）

坐这儿傻想
钱都哪儿去了？
坐这儿傻想
钱都哪儿去了？
哦，钱都给了我女人
她甭想从这儿再拿一分

昨晚出去了
买了两个鸡蛋一片火腿
昨晚出去了
买了两个鸡蛋一片火腿
账单三美元十美分
我甚至都没买果酱

那人来了
要租金
那人来了
要租金
唉，我看了抽屉
但是钱都花光了

Well, well
Ain't got no bank account
Well, well
Ain't got no bank account
Went down to start one
But I didn't have the right amount

Everything's inflated
Like a tire on a car
Everything's inflated
Like a tire on a car
Well, the man came and took my Chevy back
I'm glad I hid my old guitar

Come to me, mama
Ease my money crisis now
Come to me, mama
Ease my money crisis now
I need something to support me
And only you know how

唉，唉
没有银行户头
唉，唉
没有银行户头
下去开一个
可没有足够的钱

一切都膨胀[1]了
就像汽车的轮胎
一切都膨胀了
就像汽车的轮胎
唉，那人收走了我的雪佛兰
我很高兴把旧吉他藏起来了

到我这儿来，妈妈[2]
快来缓解我的金钱危机
到我这儿来，妈妈
快来缓解我的金钱危机
我需要支持
只有你知道怎么做

---

[1] 膨胀，与"通货膨胀"双关。
[2] 妈妈，对情人的昵称。